access to history

The Unification o
1815–70 THIRD ED TION

Robert P ce a d Andrina Stiles

HODDER
EDUCATION
AN HACHETTE UK COMPANY

Study guides revised and updated, 2008, by Sally Waller (AQA), Angela Leonard (Edexcel) and Martin Jones (OCR).

The publishers would like to thank the following individuals, institutions and companies for permission to reproduce copyright illustrations in this book: AKG-images, page 31; © Archivo Iconografico, S.A./CORBIS, page 57; www.cartoonstock.com, page 45; Getty Images, page 51; © John Madere/CORBIS, page 144; © Michael Nicholson/CORBIS, page 108; © 1990 photo Scala, Florence, page 83; © Popperfoto.com, pages 26, 111; Reproduced with the permission of Punch, Ltd., page 64, 121, 135.
The publishers would like to thank the following for permission to reproduce material in this book: Oxford, Cambridge and RSA (OCR) examinations for extracts used on pages 46, 121, 136.
The publishers would also like to thank the following: Historical Association for an extract from *Cavour* by H. Hearder, 1972; Longman for an extract from The Unification of Italy by Graham Darby, 2001; Methuen Young Books for an extract from From Vienna to Versailles by L. Seaman, 1955; National Textbook Company for an extract from *The Unification of Italy* by A. Stiles, 1986; Routledge for an extract from The Unification of Italy by John Gooch, 1986.

Although every effort has been made to ensure that website addresses are correct at time of going to press, Hodder Murray cannot be held responsible for the content of any website mentioned in this book. It is sometimes possible to find a relocated web page by typing in the address of the home page for a website in the URL window of your browser.

Orders: please contact Bookpoint Ltd, 130 Milton Park, Abingdon, Oxon OX14 4SB. Telephone: (44) 01235 827720. Fax: (44) 01235 400454. Lines are open 9.00–5.00, Monday to Saturday, with a 24-hour message answering service. Visit our website at www.hoddereducation.co.uk

© Robert Pearce and Andrina Stiles 2006
First published in 2006 by
Hodder Education,
an Hachette UK Company
338 Euston Road
London NW1 3BH

Impression number   10 9 8 7 6
Year   2010 2009

Cover photo shows the Battle of Solferino © Mary Evans Picture Library
Produced and typeset in Baskerville by Gray Publishing, Tunbridge Wells
Printed in Malta

A catalogue record for this title is available from the British Library

ISBN: 978 0 340 90701 6

Contents

Dedication

Keith Randell (1943–2002)

The *Access to History* series was conceived and developed by Keith, who created a series to 'cater for students as they are, not as we might wish them to be'. He leaves a living legacy of a series that for over 20 years has provided a trusted, stimulating and well-loved accompaniment to post-16 study. Our aim with these new editions is to continue to offer students the best possible support for their studies.

1

Introduction: The Unification of Italy

POINTS TO CONSIDER

In 1815 'Italy' was merely a geographical expression, and very few people believed that one day the peninsula would become a nation state. Yet by 1861 almost all of Italy had been unified. This chapter should be regarded as a curtain-raiser to the drama of Italian unification, providing essential background knowledge. It looks at three different periods:

- Pre-Napoleonic rule, largely by Austrian rulers
- French rule under Napoleon
- The Restored Monarchies

Finally, the chapter sketches an outline of the process by which, after 1848, 'Italy' was formed as a political entity, and of the main interpretations that have been put forward by contemporaries and historians to explain what happened. This will allow you to form a 'mental map' of the key events and ideas, enabling you to follow the next, more detailed, chapters with greater ease.

Key dates

1796   Napoleon Bonaparte invaded Italy
1815   Napoleon defeated at Waterloo
        The Congress of Vienna: Austria to be dominant in
            Italy
        The 'Restored Monarchs' began to return to their
            Italian states

1 | Pre-Napoleonic Italy

Key question
What were the main political divisions in Italy?

Around the start of the nineteenth century, many Europeans considered that Italy was the heartland of world civilisation. Twice, during the Roman Empire and at the time of the Renaissance, it had dominated Europe, first politically and then culturally. Yet the times had sadly changed, and now Italy had declined and was languishing under foreign rule or petty dictators. Italy was now more an art gallery and a museum, some believed, than a modern state.

In 1796, when Napoleon's army had overrun Italy, the peninsula had comprised a complicated patchwork of states and

Key date
Napoleon Bonaparte invaded Italy: 1796

principalities (see the map below). The main bodies of this complex mosaic were:

- The northern state of Piedmont, ruled by the House of Savoy from its capital in Turin. In 1720 the Duke of Savoy had acquired the island of Sardinia and the title of King. This joint state had originally been known as 'The Kingdom of Sardinia' or 'Sardinia-Piedmont', but in the nineteenth century was generally referred to simply as Piedmont.
- The northern state of Lombardy, which was ruled by local representatives of the Austrian Empire, supported by the Austrian army. It was one of the most advanced parts of Italy economically and its capital, Milan, had a population of around 130,000.
- Venetia, governed according to a constitution that had changed little since the Renaissance, was dominated by its local aristocracy. Austria had great influence in the area.
- The Central Duchies, of Tuscany, Modena and Parma. They were governed by their own dukes, but again Austria was very influential, so much so that they have been called **satellites** of Austria. The ruling dynasty in Tuscany, for instance, the House of Lorraine, was part of the Habsburg family, which ruled in Austria.

Satellites
Weak states
dependent on or
controlled by a
more powerful
country.

Key term

Italy c1796, showing the main regions.

Key term

Viceroy
A ruler exercising authority on behalf of a king or queen.

- The Papal States, covering most of central Italy, were governed by the Pope. Economically the region was weak, and militarily it relied on support from other Catholic countries.
- The Kingdom of Naples, ruled by the Bourbon family, constituted the largest but also the poorest region in Italy. From Naples, the largest city in Italy, the king also ruled Sicily, via a **viceroy**, which was poverty stricken. The combined kingdom was often referred to as 'The Kingdom of the two Sicilies'.

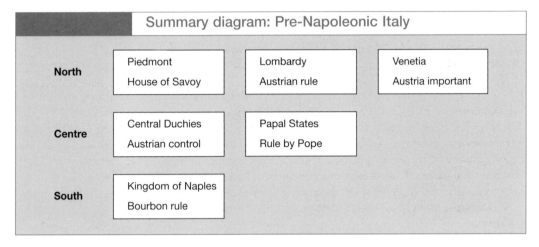

Summary diagram: Pre-Napoleonic Italy

North	Piedmont House of Savoy	Lombardy Austrian rule	Venetia Austria important
Centre	Central Duchies Austrian control	Papal States Rule by Pope	
South	Kingdom of Naples Bourbon rule		

Key question
What were the main effects of French rule in Italy?

Key figure

Napoleon Bonaparte 1769–1821
Joined the French army in 1785 and made a name for himself as a brilliant commander in wars against the British and the Austrians. He instituted a military dictatorship in France in 1799 and crowned himself Emperor, as Napoleon I, in 1804. He was forced to abdicate, after a series of military defeats, in 1814.

2 | French Rule under Napoleon

The French attacked the Kingdom of Piedmont-Sardinia in 1792, acquiring Nice and Savoy. A few years later, in 1796, **Napoleon Bonaparte** gained control of the army in Italy and, after a war with the Austrians in Lombardy, soon took over the whole peninsula. In 1805 Napoleon crowned himself King of Italy.

Napoleon made a series of changes which simplified political boundaries. In 1798 he did away with the old complicated pattern of states and divided most of the country into just four separate republics. In 1810 he divided the country again, but this time into just three parts (see the map on page 4):

- One third was annexed to France and treated as part of the French Empire. This comprised the north-west portion of Italy, including Piedmont, together with the Central Duchies and the Papal States.
- Another third became known as the Kingdom of Italy. This comprised the regions of Lombardy, Modena, Bologna, Romagna and Ferrara. Napoleon was king but his stepson ruled as viceroy.
- The remaining third was the Kingdom of Naples, but it did not include Sicily, which was now controlled by Britain, and the ruling dynasty was no longer the Bourbons. Instead Napoleon's brother, Joseph, became king.

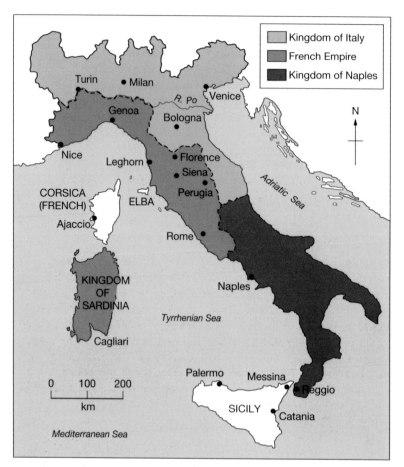

The tripartite division of Napoleonic Italy c1810.

Life under French rule

Historians are very divided over what life was like for the Italian people under French rule, not surprisingly, perhaps, since almost 20 million people then lived in the Italian peninsula. Some believe that 'Italy's experience during the period was traumatic from every point of view' and that the 'brutality and irreligion of the French soldiery' were largely to blame. Certainly a great many men were required for the French army and a great deal of money was needed to train, equip and feed the French soldiers and the Italian conscripts. No fewer than 27,000 Italian soldiers accompanied Napoleon to Russia in 1812, but only 1000, many of them badly wounded, survived to return home on foot, having lost all their horses and cannon in the campaign.

Italians deeply resented the increased conscription of their young men into the army, along with the high taxation needed to make good the loss of so many soldiers, horses and weapons. War, though, was Napoleon's life and as much as 60 per cent of tax revenue collected in Italy by the French authorities was used to fund military expenditure even in peacetime. Nevertheless, the experiences of different groups in Italy undoubtedly varied, as we can see by examining different sectors of Italian society under French rule.

Key question
What were the positive and what were the negative features of French rule in Italy?

Temporal power
The worldly authority of the Pope, as ruler of the Papal States.

Spiritual authority
The religious power of the Pope, as head of the Catholic Church.

Code Napoléon
A set of civil laws, formulated in 1804, which gave France a single legal system and attempted to promote the principle of equal rights for all citizens. (Women, it should be noted, were classified as minors not as citizens.)

The Church

The Roman Catholic Church was one body that suffered severely. Its power was greatly reduced and two Popes were actually imprisoned in France. In 1809 its **temporal power** was declared to be at an end. The Papal States were to be governed by the French and not by the Pope and his cardinals. This did not affect the Pope's **spiritual authority**, for he remained head of the Church, but by 1814 almost all monasteries had been closed down by the French. In addition, the Church lands were sold off – and not in the small lots the peasants hoped for and might have been able to buy, but in large lots to landowning noble families or to wealthy merchants from the towns who wanted to set up as landed gentry.

The wealthy

Whether the families of well-to-do noble landowners and of middle-class bankers and merchants suffered under French rule is unclear. Accounts vary widely, but many were written as memoirs long after the events they describe and so may not be entirely accurate. The families of two noblemen who later became Prime Ministers of Piedmont, Camillo Cavour and Massimo d'Azeglio, are good examples. The Cavours seem to have done well out of the purchase of Church lands, while d'Azeglio, in memoirs written nearly half a century later, complained that his family was ruined under French rule.

Urban groups

There were substantial benefits from French rule for most of the 10 per cent or so Italians who lived in towns. The majority of these were professional men and their families – well-to-do middle-class merchants, lawyers, bankers, apothecaries, doctors and government officials. Lower in the social scale, tradesmen, artisans and craftsmen also profited from the increased prosperity of the middle class as changes introduced by Napoleon brought financial and business advantages.

External customs barriers were simplified and internal trade barriers between the Italian states were swept away, weights and measures were standardised, tax collection was reorganised, new and better roads were built and transport was improved. The *Code Napoléon* was introduced nationally to replace the earlier hotchpotch of separate state laws, and new local government districts were set up along French lines. Industry was encouraged (so that France might benefit from buying cheap Italian goods) and vaccination against smallpox was made available. Street lighting in towns was introduced. At first this caused unexpected problems. It seems that in Milan this new attempt to make the streets safer at night was not appreciated: the flickering oil lamps are said to have 'quite blinded the pedestrians', making them easier targets for pickpockets and other criminals. But in the long run there were undoubted benefits.

The most important development for the future was probably the introduction by the French of a two-chamber representative government in each of the states. Many young Italian men were able to gain experience of politics and government in these 'parliaments'. Italians absorbed French ideals of liberty, equality and fraternity, and some accepted that men should be citizens of a state rather than subjects of a king. Others were trained in leadership as officers in the French army of occupation or in the **conscripted**, well-trained Italian army of 80,000 men. These experiences were to stand both groups in good stead in the years of revolution and nationalist struggle.

The peasants

Meanwhile peasant families, who made up between 80 and 90 per cent of Italians in the early nineteenth century, continued to live a life far removed from that of the **élite** middle-class families of Piedmont or Tuscany, or the old aristocracy of southern Italy. Italian peasant families, ignored in their lifetime and long dismissed by historians as uneducated, unimportant, non-political and unworthy of study, are often now the focus of new research.

Key question
In what ways were the peasants affected by French rule?

Marriage customs

The Italian historian Marzio Barbagli has made an intensive study of the ages at which men and women married within the peasant communities in different parts of Italy and whether they set up their own home or lived with parents. In the rural south, Italian couples married comparatively young, women on average at 19 years of age and men shortly before they were 25. They were able to do this because the parents of a girl about to marry often supplied her with '**dowry** gifts', including a bed, clothes and linen. Where the families were too poor this was usually impossible. Nevertheless, a landless labourer would often marry and set up a household 'with a few pence of his own, a few from his wife and whatever he can borrow and at once start a family'.

In Sardinia, because her father did not give a dowry, a girl had to make with her own hands the things she needed. As she had very little time during the day, the work took a long while to complete and the age at which she was free to marry was consequently higher than elsewhere. Many young men were never able to marry at all because it was customary in some areas that the head of the family must remain a bachelor.

Occupations

Most peasants lived as they had always done, in dark, damp, poorly furnished cottages that they shared with their livestock for warmth at night. They tilled their fields with wooden ploughs, perhaps with the help of a horse, perhaps not, and carried their crops home on their backs, since over most of rural Italy a wheeled cart was unknown. Unfortunately, the most easily and therefore most commonly grown crop was maize. When eaten in large quantities as the staple diet it results in vitamin deficiency and gives rise to the terrible disease **pellagra**. In one year in the early nineteenth century 95,000 cases were reported among peasants in Venetia alone.

Key terms

Conscripted
Forcibly enlisted into the army.

Élite
The most important and influential groups in a society, usually those who are wealthy and well educated.

Dowry
Property or money presented by a bride or her family to her husband.

Pellagra
A disease causing skin complaints, diarrhoea and madness that often ends in suicide.

Rather than remain almost permanently on the verge of starvation and the prey of bad weather and failed crops, many young men left the family farms, took to the hills and became bandits. Many young women moved for work into the town, where they often found instead diseases such as typhoid, cholera, diphtheria and tuberculosis spread by overcrowding, with as many as 80 people in a house, a non-existent sewage system and a lack of clean drinking water.

Many women in both town and country discovered, if they did manage to find a job or to obtain work which could be done at home, that it was impossible to keep their babies and often abandoned them at the nearest **foundling** hospital. There a container set in the front door allowed a baby to be left with some sort of identification. If conditions improved the mother might return and reclaim her child at a later date, months or sometimes years later. By then the child might no longer be alive, for the death rate in foundling hospitals was high.

If peasant women remained in the countryside, they were expected not only to help their husbands in the fields and to feed and care for their families, but also to make a little money at home. Often they would become **outworkers** for some urban merchant by spinning or weaving, sewing shirts or, with the help of the children, raising silk worms and reeling off the silk from the resulting cocoons for the major Italian manufacturing industry of silk weaving.

Key terms

Foundling
An infant abandoned by its mother and cared for by others.

Outworkers
Those provided with work by a factory but doing it at home.

Key question
What was the significance of French rule for nationalist movements in Italy?

Conclusion

The effects of French rule in Italy were paradoxical. Many educated Italians were inspired by the ideas the French brought with them, some wanting to imitate France by modernising Italy and even founding an Italian nation state. On the other hand, French rule all too often fell lamentably short of the standards it aspired to. Heavy-handed French imperialism inspired a wish in many Italians to overthrow French domination. The question was, could this be achieved? If so, would it be done by peaceful methods, including debate and agreement, or would violence be needed?

Research on the Italian peasantry has revealed that historians' focus on 'high politics' and on the process that led to unification can easily mislead us into thinking that this preoccupied most Italians. But such was certainly not the case. For most Italians life was a constant struggle for survival, and politics seemed entirely irrelevant. Two key questions arise from this:

- Could nationalists mobilise the peasant masses to take an interest in unification? If so, nationalism might well develop into a force to be reckoned with.
- Could politicians – either before or after unification – take the constructive measures that would raise the standard of living for ordinary Italians? If not, a true democracy was unlikely to evolve.

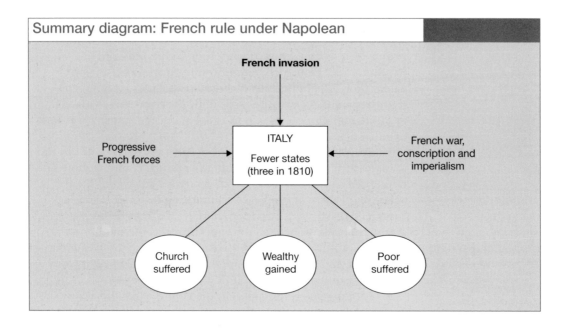

Summary diagram: French rule under Napolean

French invasion

↓

ITALY
Fewer states
(three in 1810)

Progressive French forces →

← French war, conscription and imperialism

Church suffered

Wealthy gained

Poor suffered

3 | The Restored Monarchies

In 1815 French control of Italy came to an end with the defeat of Napoleon at Waterloo and his final exile to St Helena. All his boundary changes were set aside. The European powers, meeting at the Congress of Vienna, decided to return Italian state boundaries to more or less what they had been in the middle of the eighteenth century before Napoleon's arrival.

The main divisions of Italy would be as follows (see the map on page 9):

- In the north, Piedmont was restored to its king, Victor Emmanuel I. His territory was now enlarged to include Savoy, recovered from France, and also **Genoa**.
- Elsewhere in the north, Lombardy and Venetia were now joined together, under a new viceroy controlled from Vienna.
- The Central Duchies (Tuscany, Modena and Parma) were returned to the control of Austrian-appointed local rulers. For instance, Ferdinand III, the brother of the Austrian Emperor, became the Grand Duke of Tuscany.
- The Papal States were returned to the control of the Pope, although now Austrian armed forces were to be stationed there.
- In the south, King Ferdinand I was restored to the throne, controlling both Naples and Sicily. He was in theory independent, but he accepted that no important change would be made to his government without Austria's approval.

Key question
Was life for Italians better or worse under the Restored Monarchies than under the French?

Napoleon was defeated at Waterloo: June 1815

The Congress of Vienna returned Italy to its old rulers: 1815

Key dates

Genoa
The Vienna Settlement of 1815 gave Piedmont control of the former republic of Genoa. This was of great commercial benefit to Piedmont, as Genoa was an important port. But the Genoese were far from impressed, resenting the loss of their former political and commercial independence.

Key term

Italy after the
Congress of Vienna,
1815.

Map labels:

Geneva

SAVOY

FRANCE

HABSBURG KINGDOM OF LOMBARDO-VENETIA

Milan

Turin

PIEDMONT

Parma

Genoa

Nice

Venice

Modena

Florence

TUSCANY

PAPAL STATES

Adriatic Sea

N

KINGDOM OF SARDINIA-PIEDMONT

ELBA

CORSICA

Rome

SARDINIA

Tyrrhenian Sea

NAPLES

Naples

KINGDOM OF THE TWO SICILIES

0 100 200
km

Palermo

SICILY

Mediterranean Sea

Key figure

Prince Clemens Metternich 1773–1859
The dominant figure in the Austrian government from 1809 to 1848. He was determined to suppress liberal and nationalist movements and regarded dominance in Italy as essential to Austria's security.

Key date

The 'Restored Monarchs' began to return to their Italian states: 1815

What all this amounted to was an Italy largely controlled by Austria, as the Congress of Vienna had intended. The Congress had decided that, after a period of upheaval, stability was needed. That meant a return to the old ways. Above all, future French invasions had to be prevented, and that meant Austria must control most of the peninsula. This was very much in accordance with the plans of the Austrian Chancellor, **Metternich**, one of the key figures in the Congress. He wished 'to extinguish the spirit of Italian unity and ideas about constitutions'. As he said at the time, 'Italian affairs do not exist'.

Old rulers return

In 1815 the old ruling families were clamouring to be allowed to return to Italy from the exile in which most of them had lived out the Napoleonic era. They were anxious, now that their old state boundaries had been restored, to return to their previous lifestyles. It was not long before kings, princes, dukes and duchesses were finding their way back to Italy.

Their return was generally welcomed by the landowning nobility of the countryside, by the well-to-do middle class in the towns and, especially, by the Pope and the Roman Catholic

Church. For all these it signalled a welcome return to the old ways.

Yet with very few exceptions the peasants, who made up about 90 per cent of the population, neither knew nor cared what was happening outside their own villages. Whether it was the French, the Austrians or a Restored Monarch who ruled was of little or no importance to them in their struggle for survival.

Life under the Restored Monarchs

The **Restored Monarchs** have long been seen by historians as trying to turn the clock back to pre-Napoleonic times in an attempt to return to absolute government. Hence they have been judged as essentially **reactionary**. Their alliance with the Church, and also their general friendliness with the Habsburg government in Austria, has led historians to write off the Restored Monarchs as old-fashioned and unprogressive.

Between 1815 and 1861, when Italy was unified, the social disturbances and revolutions that took place were until recently described by historians as a struggle between progress (working to make Italy a united independent nation, often through membership of secret societies) and reaction (out-of-date absolute rule, brutal oppression and a general opposition to popular nationalist ambitions for Italian unity and independence).

New research by **revisionist historians**, however, suggests a different situation. They argue that in only a few states and on only a few occasions did Restoration governments behave in a reactionary way. Most of the opposition, revisionists say, came not because popular demands for a part in government were being ignored: the real trouble was just the opposite. It was not because monarchs were keeping too much power in their own hands, but because they were modernising their governments and setting up a central administration to carry out everyday business. Admittedly most Restoration governments used censorship, police surveillance and military force to deal with unrest, but so did most other European states in the early nineteenth century.

Examples of **progressive** Restoration governments include the following:

- In Tuscany, Ferdinand III was no reactionary. He improved education, reorganising the universities of Pisa and Siena and spending more on the education of girls. He also expanded health facilities and refused to allow the **Jesuits** entry to the Duchy. Above all, he allowed freedom of expression to a degree not seen elsewhere in Italy. Hence the journal *Antologia*, founded in 1821, began to flourish. Its contributors included some of the great intellectual figures of the century, including the leading Italian nationalist, Giuseppe Mazzini. As a result, Florence became, in most people's judgement, the cultural and in some ways the political centre of Italy. Ferdinand would probably have granted a constitution if Metternich had allowed him to.

Key question
Did life for Italians change under the Restored Monarchs?

Key terms

Restored Monarchs
The rulers whom the Congress of Vienna allowed to return to Italy.

Reactionary
Favouring a return to previous political conditions and being opposed to political progress.

Revisionist historians
Those who disagree with generally accepted historical interpretations and seek to overturn them by arguing differently.

Progressive
Forward-looking, favouring reform.

Jesuits
Members of the Society of Jesus, a religious order founded in the sixteenth century, who were feared for their extreme loyalty to the Papacy.

- In Parma, Duchess Marie-Louise was, by the standards of the time, another enlightened ruler. She repealed the *Code Napoléon* (see page 5) but replaced it with something very similar and would allow no policy of blind reaction.

There were, however, four states that were indeed backward looking: Piedmont, Modena, the Papal States and Naples.

Piedmont

When King Victor Emanuel I returned to Piedmont in 1815 he set out to turn the clock back to pre-Napoleonic days. Middle-class officials in the government and law courts, and non-noble officers in the army who had been appointed under Napoleon, were dismissed and replaced by members of the old noble families. In addition, the *Code Napoléon* was done away with and the former eighteenth-century laws, with their special privileges for the nobility, were restored. The king even went to the lengths of ploughing up parks and tearing down gaslights because they had been introduced by the French.

The old customs barriers were reintroduced, the use of the new roads built by the French was actively discouraged, control of education was handed back to the Roman Catholic Church, and the Jesuits, who had been exiled by Napoleon, were invited to return. Nobles were given back their lands and, at the same time, the old anti-Jewish laws restricting ownership of property were reintroduced and Jews were once again ordered to remain in the **ghettos** instead of being allowed to move freely about the country.

Modena

The return of the Habsburg Duke Francis IV to Modena in 1815 heralded a similar attempt to return to the pre-Napoleonic era. Italians holding government offices under Napoleon were removed, being replaced by members of the nobility. The Jesuits returned. Francis also married the daughter of Victor Emmanuel of Piedmont, a man whose rule he much admired. He hated all **liberals**, and yet he also had quarrels with Austria, which confined his rule to the small duchy of Modena.

The Papal States

A series of hardline Popes, known collectively as 'the zealots', between them established a tight hold on government, education, culture and politics within the Papal States.

All central and local government was in the hands of priests, the **lay population** having almost no say in what happened. The *Code Napoléon* was abolished, censorship was strictly imposed and all opposition forcibly repressed. The **Inquisition** sometimes used torture against those whose ideas were deemed too modern. It was even forbidden to say that the earth revolved round the sun, since the Church decreed otherwise! Religious persecution increased, and toleration of any other belief than Roman Catholic doctrine was forbidden.

Key terms

Ghettos
Special quarters in Italian towns outside which Jews were forbidden to live.

Liberals
Members of the élite who wanted progressive change: often constitutional government, the guarantee of individual freedoms and free trade.

Lay population
People who are not members of the clergy.

Inquisition
A much-feared tribunal for prosecuting and punishing heresy, founded in the thirteenth century.

Jews, in particular, came in for harsh treatment. Their children could be taken away to be brought up as Catholics by the Church if it could be shown, or sometimes even if it was alleged, that anyone – a friend, a servant, or a relative – had baptised them secretly. The seizing from his home in the ghetto of a young Jewish boy, Edgar Mortara, who may or may not have been baptised by a simple-minded servant girl, created a great sensation which helped, despite the opposition of the Pope, to bring the practice of kidnapping to an end.

Developments in communication were hindered by the Pope's refusal to allow railways and the telegraph within his lands.

In this period the Papal States had the unenviable reputation of being the most backward and oppressive of all the Italian states. They were also among the most economically poor, with unemployment and begging being common.

Naples

The Bourbon king, Ferdinand I, returned as King of Naples in 1815. The following year he cancelled the Sicilian constitution of 1812, which had allowed the people a say in government. In future, he declared, Sicily would be governed as part of the kingdom of Naples. Liberals and **radicals** joined together to call for a new constitution, but the king refused their demand.

In Naples too, Ferdinand's rule was oppressive, cruel and reactionary, and there were very few economic successes that perhaps might have compensated for the stifling political atmosphere. In 1820, in Naples and Sicily, there began the first of a long, drawn-out series of revolutions (which are dealt with in Chapter 2).

Radicals
Reformers who wanted greater change than the liberals, including the overthrow of monarchies.

Key term

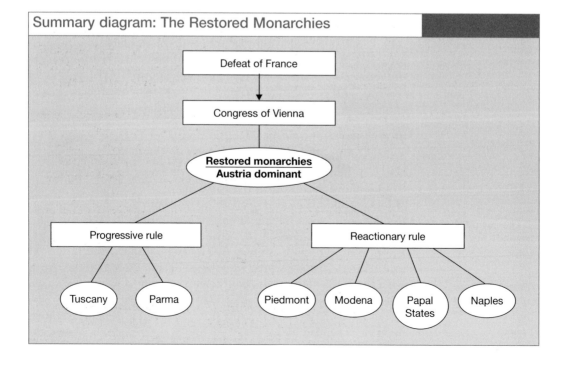

Summary diagram: The Restored Monarchies

- Defeat of France
  - Congress of Vienna
    - **Restored monarchies Austria dominant**
      - Progressive rule
        - Tuscany
        - Parma
      - Reactionary rule
        - Piedmont
        - Modena
        - Papal States
        - Naples

4 | Unification: A Brief Overview

Key question
What were the basic 'ingredients' that produced unification?

Napoleon had said, 'Italy is one nation. Unity of customs, language and literature must at a period more or less distant unite her inhabitants under one government, and Rome without doubt will be chosen by the Italians as their capital'.

In the early 1800s this scenario was only a dream for Italian nationalists. By the 1860s the dream had come true. How it happened is the subject of the rest of this book.

Nationalism

Key question
Why did nationalism grow in nineteenth-century Italy?

Several factors were involved in the process of unification. One was the growth of national feeling. In the period after French rule, intellectuals became more interested in Italian history and culture, gaining more confidence that Italians were in fact a cultural nation. Philosophers decided around this time that language embodied the distinctive essence of a national group – the special spirit that bound people together and made them a nation, distinct from outsiders. Admittedly there was no single Italian language, but neither was there quite the linguistic variety in the Italian peninsula that some have believed. Instead, the variations were rather **dialects** than entirely new languages. In addition, one of these dialects – Tuscan Italian – was easily the most popular form of written language.

Key term
Dialect
The form of a language found in a particular region.

Yet several important issues were unresolved, all relating to the strength of Italian nationalism:

- Could local discontent, especially with the existing rulers, be converted into enthusiasm for a new Italian state?
- Could Italian nationalism override loyalty to a particular region or state?
- Just how much mass support could Italian nationalism generate? Would it involve only the small intellectual élite, or would it receive support from industrial workers and peasants? The latter constituted the great majority of Italian people, and nationalism would be all the weaker if it could not generate truly mass support.
- How many nationalist parties and groups would there be, and what would they stand for? Should a new Italian state be a republic or a monarchy? Clearly the more alternatives there were, the less cohesion and the less strength the nationalist movement would have. Unless there was unity, there could be no real strength.
- Would nationalism be strong enough to overcome the existing, mostly Austrian, rulers in Italy, or would the Italians need to enlist international support to overcome the stranglehold of Austria on the Italian peninsula?

Revolutions

Three sets of revolutions occurred in Italy: in 1820–1, 1831–2 and 1848–9. The demands of the rebels in 1820 and 1831 were moderate protests against oppressive rule rather than attempts to forge an Italian nation. They also failed totally, owing to divisions among themselves, lack of mass support and the might of the Austrian army. But in 1848 there was initial success, as the existing rulers often fled their territories. There was also a nationalist aspect to the revolutions. A republic was set up by nationalists in Rome, and Charles Albert, the King of Piedmont – the one ruler in Italy who was definitely an Italian – declared war on Austria and called for independence for an Italian Union. Some believed that the Pope might be made head of a federation of Italian states.

Yet these hopes were soon dashed. French forces restored papal rule in Rome, and the Austrians defeated Piedmontese forces on the battlefield. It was becoming clear that nationalist movements were too weak and too divided among themselves, and that allies were needed to overcome Austrian control. It was also becoming clear that it was the hitherto politically backward state of Piedmont that had the best chance of spearheading the unification of Italy.

Piedmont and unification

Piedmont, under its king Victor Emmanuel II and its prime minister Camillo Cavour, grew stronger in the 1850s; and in 1859, having enlisted the help of the French Emperor, Napoleon III, it defeated Austria and formed the Kingdom of Northern Italy. Here was a successful measure of unification, although it was not altogether easy to say whether it was a result of Italian nationalism or Piedmontese imperialism.

The process might have stopped there, as many in the north looked upon the south of the peninsula as a backward and essentially foreign land. But Giuseppe Garibaldi – a swashbuckling military leader who was determined that the whole of Italy should be free and united – successfully wrested both Sicily and Naples from their Austrian king and, in 1860, handed them over to Victor Emmanuel. The Kingdom of Italy was formed in 1861, very much on the model of Piedmont; and soon the rest of the peninsula was added, Venice in 1866 and Rome, which became the new capital, in 1870, both as a result of diplomacy and Prussia's wars.

Interpretations

How do we make sense of the events that comprised Italian unification? One popular explanation has been to stress nationalism, the force of which produced the ***Risorgimento***, a revival or awakening in Italy amounting to a national rebirth. Such an interpretation implies that Italy came into being not as a result of war and diplomacy and the actions of foreigners but, essentially, as a result of its own growth and the abilities and actions of Italians.

Many writers from the 1860s onwards have favoured the notion of *Risorgimento*, insisting that the timing of unification and the precise form that it took were determined by the exploits of Cavour and Garibaldi, the two greatest heroes of nineteenth-

Key term

Risorgimento
The word first came into use at the end of the eighteenth century and means 'resurgence' or 'rebirth'. Those who first used it suggested that Italian unification would be a noble and heroic affair, paralleling glorious episodes in Italian history such as the Roman Empire and the Renaissance.

Key question
What is the fundamental division between historians on what caused Italian unification?

century Italian history. Their successful partnership brought the *Risorgimento* to a glorious conclusion. The essence of this interpretation is that Italians co-operated, and thus earned their own liberation from oppressive rule.

Most modern historians, however, especially from Britain, are far more sceptical. They cannot see the nationalist movement proceeding to an almost preordained and glorious unification, especially since the new Kingdom of Italy performed badly after 1861, and indeed succumbed to Mussolini's Fascist movement in the 1920s. They note continued divisions between the different nationalist groups during the 1850s and 1860s, the necessity for foreign help in defeating Austria, especially from France, and tend to see the unification of 1860 stemming not from the co-operation of Cavour and Garibaldi but from their rivalries and indeed hostility. In short, they emphasise **contingent** factors more than those Italian historians who still believe that the *Risorgimento* explains unification.

Key term

Contingent
Subject to chance and to the effects of the unforeseen.

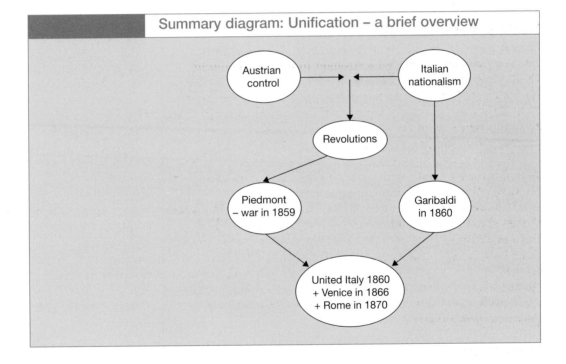

Summary diagram: Unification – a brief overview

Study Guide: AS Question

In the style of Edexcel

To what extent was lack of popular support the *main* obstacle to Italian unification in the period 1830–49? (30 marks)

Exam tips

The cross-references are intended to take you straight to the material that will help you to answer the question.

You would have 40 minutes to answer this question, or one like it, and therefore your factual knowledge needs to be sufficient for you to write several pages. Hence you could only tackle this question fully after you have read Chapter 2 of this book. Nevertheless it will help you to digest the information in the current chapter, and practise the vital skill of logical thinking, if you at least make an essay plan at this stage.

First you have to address the issue of popular support, or the lack of it. Questions you might address include:

- Was there mass discontent in Italy (see pages 6–7)?
- Was this channelled into political movements (see pages 13–15)?
- How important was mass participation in the revolutions of 1831–2 and 1848–9 (see pages 13–14)?

Then you should examine the barriers to unification. If they were weak, then perhaps small numbers of middle-class liberals or radicals could overcome them and unite Italy without generating mass support. But, of course, if the barriers were strong, then the nationalists were more likely to need the backing of the masses. Questions you might ask include:

- How was Italy divided by the Congress of Vienna (see pages 8–9)?
- How strong were these divisions? Here you might ask who ruled the individual states and whether they had the support of Austria or of the Catholic Church (see pages 8–9). Some precise information from the revolutions might be useful here.

Then you could look at the forces of nationalism in 1830–49 and ask whether their lack of success seemed to be due to a lack of popular support. Relevant questions include:

- How important were regional identities (see pages 10–11)?
- How many 'nationalist' movements were there by 1849? Are you sure they were really nationalist?

Next, you might consider what other barriers there were. The main one is lack of foreign support (see page 14).

Finally, do not forget to sum up the relative importance of the lack of popular support as an obstacle to unification. Here you must summarise your view as clearly as possible. Do you think it was the main obstacle? Might unification have been achieved if far more people had wanted it? Or would mass support have only been crucial only if, first, a single focus for Italian nationalism had existed? Or was mass support irrelevant in view of the might of the Austrian army? Perhaps the lack of French military support was far more crucial?

2 *Risorgimento* and Revolution 1815–49

POINTS TO CONSIDER

This chapter covers a long and important period. It begins by examining:

- The state of politics in 1815, including
- The secret societies that existed

It then focuses on the key events of the period, in particular:

- The revolutions of 1820–1
- The revolutions of 1831–2
- The revolutions of 1848–9, including the Roman Republic

You should aim to understand what the revolutions were about and why, by 1849, so little had actually been achieved. Also, you must be familiar with the major nationalist figures of this period, including:

- Giuseppe Mazzini, a key figure in the *Risorgimento*
- Other possible nationalist leaders, including Pope Pius IX

Key dates

1820–1		Revolutions
1830	June	Fighting in the streets of Paris led Charles X to abdicate
1831		Mazzini founded 'Young Italy'
1846		Pius IX elected as Pope
1848–9		Revolutions
1848	March 13	The fall of Metternich
	July 24	Charles Albert defeated by Austria at the battle of Custoza
1849	February	Founding of the Roman Republic
	June	Ending of the Roman Republic
1849	March 23	Charles Albert defeated at the battle of Novara

1 | Italian Politics in 1815

There were a number of political groups in Italy in 1815, each having different hopes and aims.

Liberals

Liberals believed that the people had the right to some say in government and that this was best done through a representative assembly or parliament elected by property owners. Liberals were also concerned with establishing a rule of law which guaranteed certain rights, such as a fair trial, and certain freedoms, such as free speech for all citizens. They were generally non-violent, mainly middle class, and were against both an **absolute monarchy** and a **republican democracy**. They favoured instead a **constitutional monarchy**.

Radicals

Radicals were much more extreme in their views. They wanted social reforms and a fairer distribution of wealth and were often prepared to use violence as a way to obtain their goals. Many of them were members of revolutionary secret societies and believed that political power should lie with the people, not with a parliament unless it were elected by all men and not just by property owners. There was at this time little thought of giving a vote to peasants or to women, since both of these groups were believed to be incapable of taking an intelligent interest in politics. Radicals had many disagreements with the liberals, but at least both groups were opposed to the Restored Monarchies.

Nationalists

Nationalists believed that people of the same race, language, culture and tradition should be united in an independent nation of their own. It should have clear geographical boundaries and not be subject to control by any other nation. Many nationalists went further and wanted a republic instead of a monarchy. Liberals and radicals both supported nationalism and unification as the way forward for Italy, even though they did not agree on whether the means to achieve this aim should be peaceful or violent. There was also widespread disagreement about whether the whole of the Italian peninsula, or merely part of it, should be unified.

Metternich's view

Metternich (see page 9) adopted an entirely negative stance, being totally opposed to nationalism, liberalism and radicalism. He had no intention of allowing such dangerous ideas to spread, as they would undermine not just Austrian control over Italy but perhaps the whole state of Austria, which was not a nation state but the family property of the Habsburg family, containing many different cultural and ethnic groups. Hence he saw the need to maintain the Italian jigsaw of separate states ruled by absolute monarchs: 'Italy' as a united nation should continue not to exist.

Key question
What political groups existed in Italy after the defeat of Napoleon, and what did each believe?

Key terms

Absolute monarchy
A political system under which a monarch rules without a constitution that limits his powers and without a parliament whose agreement is needed for the making of laws.

Republican democracy
A system under which an elected government controls the affairs of a state, and in which there is no monarch, even as a figurehead.

Constitutional monarchy
A system under which a king is bound by certain agreed restrictions on his power set out in a written document (the constitution).

Key question
Why did the Austrian Chancellor oppose nationalism in Italy?

In 1815 there were no 'Italians', he insisted, only Neapolitans, Piedmontese, Tuscans and the rest, and that was how it should stay. Hence Italy would be weak, divided and easily controlled by Austria.

Metternich was not alone in these beliefs. Many intelligent, well-educated men saw nothing but difficulties in the way of unity between the Italian states, believing that local loyalties were still more important to the people of the peninsula than dreams of national unity. Hence the Piedmontese ambassador to Russia wrote about the possible take-over of Genoa by Piedmont in 1818 that perhaps the Piedmontese and the Genoans could not mix, 'separated as they are by ancient and ingrained hatred'.

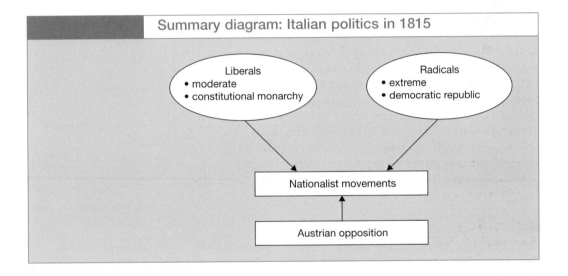

Summary diagram: Italian politics in 1815

2 | Secret Societies

Key question
What did the secret societies hope to achieve, and why did they have only limited success?

In 1820, when revolutions broke out first in Sicily and then in Naples and Piedmont, secret societies played an important part. These societies are thought to have developed from eighteenth-century **freemasonry** where men formed themselves into groups pledged to mutual protection with secret passwords and semi-religious rituals. The Church viewed these groups with grave suspicion as anti-Catholic and as a danger to the established social order. In the 1790s similar groups whose main purpose was to drive out the French had sprung up all over Italy. After 1815 their aims changed to overthrowing the Restored Monarchs and to driving out the Austrians.

Key term

Freemasonry
A secret fraternity providing fellowship and mutual assistance.

Membership
The societies attracted a wide variety of members: army officers, students, lawyers, teachers and doctors, all well educated and

mostly middle class. A few noblemen also joined but peasants and workers were almost unknown. The majority of members were patriotic, enthusiastic and daring. Many were idealists, some were dreamers, a few were rogues and criminals; some wanted to be leaders and were happy to risk their lives in wild adventures and impossible missions.

The great weakness of the societies was their unwillingness to act together and their lack of an overall organisation. Most societies were small and scattered. Sometimes they did work together, but much more often they operated on their own and, because of their emphasis on secrecy, historians are still not sure how many members they had or how successful they were.

The *Carbonari*

Far and away the best known and most important of the societies was the *Carbonari*. They were particularly active in southern Italy, especially in Naples, where they are thought to have had about 60,000 members. This was about five per cent of the adult male population, and the government of Naples became worried enough to order the suppression of the society. Their efforts failed and membership of the *Carbonari* went on rising. It is known that they had elaborate rituals and swore unquestioning obedience to their leaders.

Unlike many of the other societies, this one was not particularly anti-Catholic, and although some of its members planned armed revolution and the overthrow of the existing social order, they were not committed republicans. Often their aims in fact were surprisingly mild ones. In Piedmont they hoped to establish a constitutional monarchy, with a king having only limited power. Similarly in Naples, they did not want to replace the king with a republic, but just to persuade him to grant a constitution.

Key term

Carbonari
Means 'charcoal burners' in Italian (the singular being *Carbonaro*), and it has been suggested that the earliest members were men who sold charcoal for domestic fuel. Soon, however, middle-class members predominated.

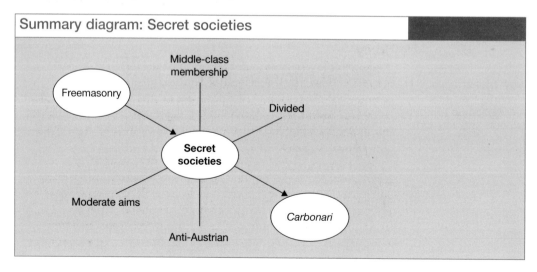

Summary diagram: Secret societies

- Freemasonry
- Middle-class membership
- Divided
- Secret societies
- Moderate aims
- Anti-Austrian
- Carbonari

Key question
Why did the
revolutions take
place?

3 | The Revolutions of 1820–1

Naples

The 1820 revolutions began in Naples where, in 1818, King
Ferdinand had greatly increased the Church's power to censor
books, newspapers and magazines. This angered the middle class,
lawyers and teachers in particular, because freedom of speech was
being made impossible. As Ferdinand was short of money he cut
back on public spending, halted works such as road and harbour
improvements and reduced still further what little education was
available to the people. Poverty, corrupt government and
restrictions on personal freedom became general.

In January 1820 news of a revolution in Spain encouraged the
Carbonari and the liberals in Naples to take action. Led by a priest
and supported by 100 junior officers and soldiers from the
cavalry, 30 *Carbonari* members advanced on the town of Avellino
and a widespread uprising soon took place. The attempt by the
government troops to round up the rebels was very half-hearted,
particularly after one of the commanding officers, General
Guglielmo Pepe, led one infantry and two cavalry regiments to
join the rebel army with himself at the head of what had now
become a revolution.

In July, King Ferdinand promised to meet the rebels' demands
for a constitution like that granted in Spain in 1812. This had
given the vote to all adult males, limited the king's power, and
abolished many noble and clerical privileges. King Ferdinand
swore to abide by such an arrangement faithfully: 'Omnipotent
God – if I lie, do thou at this moment annihilate me.' For a time
it looked as if the revolution had been a success, especially when
the revolutionaries led by General Pepe marched into the city of
Naples and were received by the king. A new government was
appointed, Pepe was put in charge of the army and the *Carbonari*
gained large numbers of recruits.

Sicily

While all this was going on another and separate revolt had
begun in Sicily, the other half of Ferdinand's kingdom, where the
people were determined to fight for independence from Naples.
Sicily had been forcibly united with Naples in 1815, and Sicilians
felt that Ferdinand's government was concentrating on Naples
and neglecting their island's needs.

Agricultural prices had fallen sharply, with disastrous
consequences for the Sicilian peasants, who found themselves
getting more and more into debt. As a result, riots took place in
Palermo, the island's capital. There were demands for a
constitution, government offices were burned down, prisoners
were released and the Neapolitan governor was sent home by
boat as the revolutionaries took over the city.

Failure in Naples and Sicily

In Naples the first meeting of the newly elected parliament took place in October 1820. Its members were middle-class professional men, lawyers, bankers and merchants, along with a few noblemen, some priests, but, of course, no peasants or women. Members discussed what had happened in Sicily and agreed that at all costs the island must remain part of the Kingdom of Naples. The island must not be allowed to declare independence and must be brought to heel, by Neapolitan armed force if necessary. Here was a dangerous division of revolutionary forces.

The Austrian Chancellor, Metternich, was greatly disturbed that the Neapolitan revolution had apparently been so successful. He did not approve of revolutions – they were unsettling events that disturbed the peace, not only of the state in which they happened, but also in neighbouring states. Therefore, he argued, it was only right for the Great Powers (Austria, Prussia and Russia) to meet and if necessary take action to suppress such disturbances wherever they occurred.

In 1821 the King of Naples was invited to attend one such meeting, at Laibach. There Ferdinand declared that he had been forced to grant the constitution out of fear and asked for Austria to help him to restore his absolute rule. Metternich did not have to be asked twice. He was delighted to intervene. In March 1821, therefore, the Austrian army entered the city of Naples, despite brave resistance led by General Pepe. Severe reprisals were meted out to the citizens indiscriminately by the Austrian authorities. Arrests, imprisonments and executions became so common that even Metternich was shocked by the savagery and ordered the dismissal of the chief of police.

In Sicily too, the old order was soon in control again. Naples recovered control over Sicily and made a future attempt at breaking away less likely by abolishing the **trade guilds** whose members had been leaders of the revolution there.

Piedmont

Piedmont was the other state that saw revolution erupt in 1820. The king, Victor Emmanuel I, had pursued a very reactionary policy since his return. He declared that the old constitution of 1770 would remain in force and could never be changed. Piedmont would therefore remain an absolute monarchy in spite of continued pressure by a small group of liberals.

When news of what was happening in Naples reached Piedmont discontent came out into the open. The *Carbonari* rapidly gained new members, and university students, army officers and liberals combined to establish a revolutionary government in the town of Alessandria, where they proclaimed their independence as the 'Kingdom of Italy' and declared war on Austria. An army mutiny in Turin, the state capital, encouraged Victor Emmanuel I to see his situation as hopeless and to abdicate.

Key question
Why did the revolutions fail?

Trade guilds
Associations of craftsmen; early forms of trade unions.

Key term

Key question
Why did revolution break out, but fail in Piedmont?

The liberals now turned for leadership to the young Charles Albert, second in line to the throne. He issued a vague proclamation praising the Spanish Constitution of 1812 as a model to be followed, and promptly appointed a new government. The main problem was that he was not the legitimate ruler. Victor Emmanuel's brother, Charles Felix, was first in line to the throne in Piedmont. He was temporarily absent from Piedmont but he soon issued a statement denouncing Charles Albert as a rebel. Charles Felix also refused to accept any change in the form of government. Charles Albert then took fright and fled from Turin, leaving the liberals to fight to defend the constitution as best they could.

At this stage Charles Felix appealed to Metternich for aid. This help came, and Austrian troops, together with troops loyal to Charles Felix, defeated the forces of the Turin liberals at the battle of Novara in 1821. Hundreds of revolutionaries went into exile. The 1820–1 revolutions were over and until 1823 Piedmont was occupied by an Austrian army.

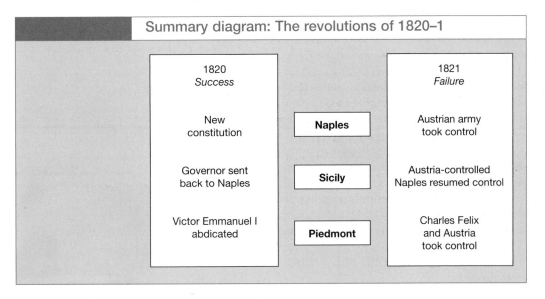

Summary diagram: The revolutions of 1820–1

1820 *Success*		1821 *Failure*
New constitution	**Naples**	Austrian army took control
Governor sent back to Naples	**Sicily**	Austria-controlled Naples resumed control
Victor Emmanuel I abdicated	**Piedmont**	Charles Felix and Austria took control

4 | The Revolutions of 1831–2

Key question
How far were the revolutions in the early-1830s simply a re-run of those a decade earlier?

Key date
Fighting in the streets of Paris led Charles X to abdicate: July 1830

In 1830 a revolution in Paris led Charles X to abdicate. The new king, Louis-Philippe, was a more liberal figure than his predecessor; indeed he was known as the 'citizen king'. Hence Italian liberals became excited by the possibility that the new French government would support revolutions in Italy. Disturbances broke out again, this time in Modena, Parma and the Papal States. In most of these places the aim was a moderate one – to persuade the local ruler to grant a constitution.

Modena and Parma

In Modena the revolt was led by Enrico Misley, the student son of a university professor. He trusted his own ruler, Duke Francis IV of Modena, to whom he revealed his plans for a united Italy, but his trust was betrayed. He was arrested in February 1831, two days before the uprising was due to begin.

Misley's arrest encouraged Duke Francis to believe that the danger was over and he went to Vienna to negotiate for Austrian help, should it be needed on some future occasion. Yet while he was away revolutionaries took over the city of Modena and set up a provisional government. This encouraged students in neighbouring Parma to organise riots and to demand a constitution from their ruler, the Duchess Marie-Louise. She fled in terror and a provisional government was established by the students. Contact with revolutionaries in Modena was at once made and a joint army commander appointed.

Yet the revolutionaries had little time to organise, for within a month Duke Francis had returned to Modena at the head of an Austrian army and quickly defeated the revolutionaries. Savage reprisals were taken and anyone suspected of supporting the rebels was imprisoned, exiled or executed. Even the wearing of a moustache or beard, supposedly signs of radicalism, could lead one to be arrested as a revolutionary. Parma was also occupied by Austrian forces, and Marie-Louise returned.

The Papal States

Similar uprisings took place in the Papal States, organised this time by the professional classes who resented the oppressive rule of the Church authorities. The papal government put up little resistance and a provisional government known as 'The Government of the Italian Provinces' was formed in Bologna in February 1831. It did not last long. Once more the power of the Austrian army proved decisive: Metternich's troops moved into the Papal States and defeated the rebels. Minor uprisings continued during 1831 and 1832 but they were fiercely suppressed by the violent and undisciplined Austrian troops.

Revolutionary success and failure 1820–32

The revolutions of 1820 and 1831 achieved very little. In Piedmont, Naples and the Papal States reactionary governments strengthened their hold with the help of Austria and by using military force.

Where revolutions were successful in ousting their rulers the success was only temporary and due more to the failure of the governments to take effective action, to the rulers' habit of running away and to their lack of military resources than to the strength of the revolutionaries. Remembering what happened in the **French Revolution** at the end of the eighteenth century, many rulers expected to be defeated. This gave the revolutionaries an early advantage, but one that they quickly lost through their failure to take united action.

The revolutions were weakened by being local affairs, concerned only with limited areas. There was little communication between the revolutionaries in the different states and even less co-operation. The revolutionary government in

Key question
Why did the revolutions fail in 1820–1 and 1831–2?

French Revolution
In the 'great revolution', beginning in 1789, the existing order was overthrown and a republic set up, Louis XVI being executed in 1793.

Key term

Bologna refused to send help to Modena, for instance. Elsewhere revolutions were not co-ordinated. They relied heavily on a network of small groups of revolutionaries set up by the *Carbonari* and other secret societies, but these were isolated units and their aims differed from place to place. Most revolutionaries were surprisingly moderate in their demands and not given to violence: usually all they were trying to achieve was the granting of a constitution to allow the people some part in government.

The revolutionary movements were mainly middle class, except in Sicily where peasants were involved. Elsewhere popular interest and support were not encouraged by the revolutionary leaders, who feared that allowing the mass of poorly educated people to join in the revolutions would lead eventually to rule by the mob. Not surprisingly, therefore, ordinary people often welcomed back their former rulers with open arms because middle-class revolutionaries did not want their involvement in politics.

In short, the revolutions had failed because the revolutionaries were divided among themselves and lacked mass support, and because they lacked outside help. It was hoped in 1831 that the French might provide military support, but when this was not forthcoming the Austrian army had an easy time of it.

By 1831 Italy still merely a geographical expression. Unification was not even on the agenda. But what of the future? Would the unsuccessful revolutions on the 1820s and 1830s, and the martyrs that had been created, inspire greater efforts? Could revolutionaries achieve greater unity and greater support? Would the international situation become more favourable?

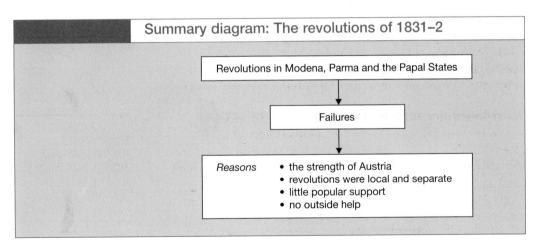

Summary diagram: The revolutions of 1831–2

Revolutions in Modena, Parma and the Papal States

Failures

Reasons
- the strength of Austria
- revolutions were local and separate
- little popular support
- no outside help

Key question
How important a figure was Mazzini in the movement for Italian unification?

5 | Giuseppe Mazzini

Despite the failure of the revolutions of the early 1830s, it was in this decade that the *Risorgimento* (see page 14) began to make some progress. This was due above all to the work of a dedicated revolutionary intellectual, Giuseppe Mazzini, dubbed by Metternich 'the most dangerous man in Europe'.

Profile: Giuseppe Mazzini 1805–72

1805	– Born in Genoa, intelligent, sensitive and physically frail
1821	– Became a nationalist after seeing Piedmontese refugee revolutionaries begging in the streets
1822–7	– Studied medicine and then law
1827	– Joined the *Carbonari*, but was betrayed in 1830. While imprisoned, he decided he must work for the independence and unification of Italy. He now became a full-time and totally committed revolutionary. He wore black as a sign of mourning for his divided and oppressed country
1831	– Moved to the south of France where he founded 'Young Italy', Italy's first real political party
1837	– Went into exile in London
1849	– Returned to Italy as head of the Roman Republic until Rome fell to the French in June 1849. Again exiled to London where he lived in poverty, writing tens of thousands of letters and hundreds of books and articles
1872	– After many years in exile he returned secretly to Italy. Died in Pisa and buried in Genoa, his birthplace

Mazzini was a highly controversial figure. His radical approach led his political enemies to criticise him as an enemy of Italy and a terrorist, and at the same time as an impractical dreamer. Yet his supporters described him as 'greatest, bravest, most heroic of Italians' and as a profound thinker. Historians' verdicts too have differed widely, partly because his thinking was complex and evolved over a long period and partly because, as an exile often under sentence of death, he often destroyed his letters. (Those that survived were written in handwriting so tiny that it served as a secret code.) What is certain, however, is that he is a key figure in the history of Italian unification.

Mazzini's ideas

It is not easy to get to grips with Mazzini's thought, and few thinkers have been so misunderstood and caricatured. Nevertheless Denis Mack Smith, in his superb biography (1994), has provided a convincing analysis of his ideas:

- Mazzini insisted that he had 'one overriding aim' and that was 'the brotherhood of people'. He believed in the equality of human beings and of races. He had contempt for **xenophobia** and imperialism.
- Yet he believed that the next stage of the world's history would be domination by nations. The political map had to be redrawn so that distinct peoples occupied their own nation-states. This

Key question
How realistic were Mazzini's ideas?

Xenophobia
Hatred of foreigners.

Key term

Karl Marx 1818–73
The socialist
philosopher and
activist who argued
that national
identities were
superficial: the
fundamental
division among
human beings was
their class
allegiance.

Federal
Possessing states
that are self-
governing in their
internal affairs.

Ambivalence
Contradictory ideas
or feelings.

stress on nationalism led **Karl Marx** to dismiss Mazzini as 'that
everlasting old ass', but Marx fatally underestimated the
importance of national allegiances.
- So, Italy had to be united.
- He did not want a **federal** Italy, which might retain the old
  foreign rulers. Instead, the whole peninsula should be
  independent, with one central government and locally elected
  authorities. *— some didn't want*
- There should be democracy and the guarantee of individual rights.
- Italy should be unified by its own efforts. He wanted to avoid
  help from France, as that might merely replace one form of
  outside domination by another.
- The ideal was that there should be unification 'from below'.
  The people should rise up against their oppressors. But if
  monarchs were prepared to fight against Austrian domination,
  they should be supported. He was not absolutely committed to
  republicanism: that was merely his ideal.
- Socially, he wanted greater equality, with an end to poverty and
  with taxation being proportional to wealth. There should be
  free and compulsory education for all and women's rights
  should be guaranteed.

Mazzini's ideas constitute a remarkably 'modern' agenda, and a
remarkably radical one in the nineteenth century. No wonder
moderate liberals in the 1840s looked upon him as dangerous.
How could they attract the support of France, while he called for
all foreign nations to stand aside from Italian affairs? How could
they generate support from wealthy figures, while he wished to
see a redistribution of wealth? How could they appeal to
individual Italian rulers, while his ideal was republicanism?
Mazzini might on occasions appeal for the support of particular
rulers, but the **ambivalence** of his thought on this issue must
surely have made them wary.

Conclusion

Were Mazzini's ideas
practical, or were they
too idealistic and
visionary?

Italy was unified, as Mazzini said it would be, and nationalism did
indeed prove a potent force in nineteenth- and twentieth-century
history. Furthermore, Mazzini's ideas inspired many disciples. Yet
history did not follow the exact pattern he hoped. As we shall see,
Italy came to be unified more 'from above' than 'from below',
much to his disgust. He was to describe the new Italian unified
state as a 'dead corpse'.
   Some may judge that an Italy unified on Mazzinian lines would
have been a more liberal, progressive and altogether preferable
state to the one that did emerge. Others will think that such a
state is pure fantasy.

'Young Italy'

How effective a
political activist was
Mazzini?

Mazzini was not merely a thinker, he aspired also to be a doer.
When Charles Albert finally became King of Piedmont in 1831,
Mazzini wrote to him about the coming revolution and invited
him to become its leader. 'Put yourself at the head of the nation;

write on your banner "Union, Liberty, Independence" … Give your name to a century'. He added privately, 'Not that I have any hopes of him', and he was right. No reply came from Charles Albert. Shortly afterwards Mazzini tried other tactics.

Mazzini founded 'Young Italy': 1831

Key date

Later in 1831, dissatisfied with the limited progress brought about by the secret societies, he founded an organisation with much clearer objectives. 'Young Italy' has been called Italy's first real political party.

He described the new party in these words:

> 'Young Italy' is a brotherhood of Italians who believe in a law of progress and duty and are convinced that Italy is destined to become one nation. They join with the intention of remaking Italy as one independent nation of freemen and equals.

Those who joined had to swear to work to make Italy 'one free independent republican nation'. Members would campaign peacefully and attempt to convince others of their views, but Mazzini also accepted that on occasions violent tactics might be necessary.

Soon Mazzini and 'Young Italy' were involved in various attempts to further the cause of unification:

- in a plan for an uprising in Naples in 1832, on the assumption that the peasants were 'a volcano about to erupt'
- in organising a mutiny in the Piedmontese army
- in a rising in Savoy
- in an attempted *coup* in Piedmont, for which, in his absence, he was condemned to death.

None of these, however, came anywhere near to success. Their main effect was probably to allow Mazzini's political enemies to spread scare stories. Metternich, for instance, insisted – quite inaccurately – that he was trying to assassinate Charles Albert.

Coup
A sudden and violent seizure of power.

Key term

Mazzini's significance

Mazzini gave tremendous impetus to Italian nationalism. No one else campaigned for long or so tirelessly in the cause of a united Italy. He spent most of his time organising a propaganda campaign to convince Italians to support the creation of a democratic, self-governing state of Italy. It is thus as an inspirational prophet that Mazzini's true significance lies. But he has two other claims to fame:

Key question
What did Mazzini achieve?

- He 'converted' many to the cause. Easily the most important of his recruits was Giuseppe Garibaldi, who involved himself in a proposed Mazzinian revolt in Genoa in 1831. The scheme failed but Garibaldi escaped before his trial and was sentenced to death in his absence. He recalled of Mazzini that 'he alone was awake when all around were slumbering'.
- Mazzini, whom many considered an impractical dreamer, became, in effect, President of Rome in 1849, and in this

position he showed highly constrictive abilities (see page 37).

Mazzini's major weakness was that his ideas were too intellectual for most people to grasp, and they were certainly too radical for most cautious, middle-class reformers. He was also absent from Italy for such long periods – totalling in all over 40 years – that he became out of touch with the situation, exaggerating the development of national identity among the bulk of Italians. It is untrue that he failed to appreciate the revolutionary potential of the peasants, but it must be admitted that he knew relatively little about them and had even less contact with them.

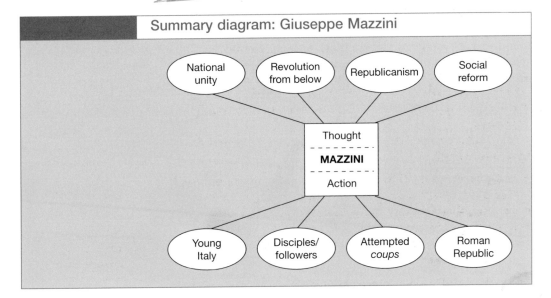

Summary diagram: Giuseppe Mazzini

6 | Alternative Strategies and Leaders

Key question
What strategies, other than the Mazzinian, existed in Italy at this time?

Mazzini was not the only revolutionary leader, and ideas very different from his were circulating among the educated élite. Two strategies focused on Piedmont and on the Pope.

Piedmont

Key question
Why did some believe that Piedmont should lead Italy?

In Piedmont moderate nationalists, taking their lead from **Cesare Balbo**, proposed that their state should lead the other Italian states in an attempt to drive out the Austrians. They argued that only Piedmont was strong enough to reclaim Lombardy and Venetia from the Austrians and rally the other Italian states into some sort of union. Proposals were put forward that Charles Albert should be the future king of a united Italy, although some believed that this new state should cover only the northern half, rather than the whole, of the peninsula.

Key figure

Cesare Balbo 1789–1853
Wrote widely on Italian history and politics. His 1844 publication, *On the Hopes of Italy*, argued that Piedmont should spearhead Italian unity.

As we shall see, in the next chapter, this strategy achieved a good deal of success, though under Charles Albert's successor as King of Piedmont.

Pope Pius IX

Another possible leader was suggested by the Piedmontese writer **Vincenzo Gioberti**. In 1843 he suggested that, as the Pope and the Catholic Church were the glories of Italy, the Italian states should form themselves into a federation with the Pope as its president. His book, *On the Moral and Civil Primacy of the Italians*, sold 5000 copies, but the bad reputation of the Papal States as oppressive and corrupt seemed too great a stumbling block for his ideas to be put into operation. However, the situation changed in 1846 with the election of a new Pope, Pius IX, who was believed to have liberal sympathies. Many were astounded that such a figure had been elected. 'We were prepared for anything', said Metternich, 'except a liberal Pope'.

Pius IX was a man of personal piety and deep faith, but emotional, excitable and with a quick temper. He was seen by many who knew him as impressionable, impulsive and unpredictable. Pius said of himself, in a letter to a previous Pope,

Key question
Why did this Pope turn out to be such an unsuitable Italian leader?

Key date

Pius IX elected as Pope: 1846

Key figure

Vincenzo Gioberti 1801–52
A Piedmontese writer and politician, was briefly prime minister of Piedmont in 1848–9 but soon retired from politics, disillusioned with Pius IX.

In this hostile cartoon from 1852 Pius is depicted as removing the mask of piety to reveal the more sinister and more scheming reality beneath.

Profile: Pope Pius IX 1792–1878

1792	– Giovanni Maria Mastai-Ferretti was born in Ancona, ninth child of a noble family with strong Church connections
1807	– Developed epilepsy; entered the Church
1819	– Became a priest, progressing to cardinal in 1845
1846	– Surprise choice as Pope on the death of Gregory XVI. Took name of Pius IX (known in Italy as Pope *Pio Nono*). Appeared to be liberal
1848 April	– Complete change of policy. Suddenly condemned Italian nationalists, rejected the *Risorgimento* and refused to allow papal troops to help drive out the Austrians. Had to escape in disguise from Rome as revolution began
1849	– **Excommunicated** all who tried to reduce temporal power of Papacy, and denounced Roman Republic
1850	– Returned to Rome. Abolished all early reforms
1861	– Catholics forbidden to have any connection with the new Kingdom of Italy
1864	– *Syllabus of Errors* published, rejecting liberalism, nationalism and other 'pernicious errors'
1870	– First Vatican Council held. Attempt to increase Pope's spiritual power, now that he had lost most of the temporal power. Papal decisions declared infallible. Freedom of religion opposed: Catholic doctrine was the only true belief
1878	– Died within a month of Victor Emmanuel II, his long-standing enemy

Key term

Excommunicated Excluded from the services and sacraments of the Catholic Church. Those who died excommunicated could not be buried by a priest or in consecrated ground, and so, it was commonly believed, would go to hell.

Pius's reputation for liberalism seemed fully justified in 1846–7. He freed 2000 political prisoners, mostly revolutionaries; he reformed education, the law and papal administration; and he gave laymen a greater share in public affairs. He also ended press censorship, allowed Jews out of the ghetto, granted Rome a constitution to replace absolute papal rule, and created the *Consulta*, an elected body to advise the Pope. Here, it seemed, was the figure that Gioberti and other nationalists had hoped for. His rapid transformation into the enemy of Italian nationalism, which was a profound blow to liberals in Italy, is extremely hard to explain.

that owing to his epilepsy he 'had a very weak memory and could not concentrate on a subject for any length of time without having to worry about his ideas getting terribly confused'. He was very easily influenced by stronger personalities and was described by the British Ambassador in 1860 as having 'an amiable but weak mind'.

Pius is remembered today for the length of his reign and for his firm stand on Catholic doctrine – and for his amazing transformation on the issue of Italian unification. The man who initially seemed to be a liberal turned out to be a reactionary.

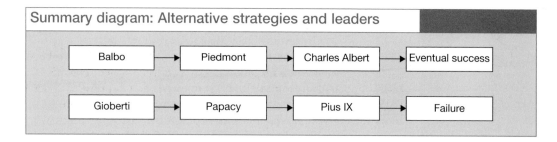

Summary diagram: Alternative strategies and leaders

Balbo → Piedmont → Charles Albert → Eventual success

Gioberti → Papacy → Pius IX → Failure

7 | The Revolutions of 1848–9

Origins

The Pope's reforms in 1848 and early 1849 set an example to other states and their rulers. In Piedmont and Tuscany, press censorship was abolished and proposals were made for a joint **customs union** with the Papal States. Even Austrian-controlled Lombardy became restless, worrying Metternich who acted swiftly to preserve Austrian control in northern Italy by making new treaties with Modena and Parma and by strengthening the Austrian **garrison**.

There was a chorus of discontent in Italy that was becoming ever louder. Liberals were calling for constitutions, government reforms and political freedom, while nationalists demanded independence from Austria and some measure of Italian unity.

The situation became more acute owing to economic problems. About 90 per cent of the population of Italy worked on the land and the Italian economy was based almost entirely on agriculture. There was little industry in the north and almost none in the south of the country. When the harvests failed in 1846 and 1847, therefore, problems multiplied not only for the peasants but also for those in the towns. Shortages of wheat and maize meant high prices, wages did not rise to meet the increased costs, and peasants and others could not afford to feed their families. The result was an outbreak of revolutions.

The course of the revolutions

Success in Sicily

Problems became acute first in Sicily, where Ferdinand II, King of Naples, had initially offered a better life for Sicilians by making reforms and appointing a viceroy to see that the reforms were carried out. These did not last and a period of repression coinciding with an outbreak of cholera left Sicilians in a desperate state.

In January 1848 notices were posted up in Palermo, the island's capital:

> Sicilians! the time for prayers is past; peaceful protests and demonstrations have all been useless. Ferdinand, King of Naples, has treated them all with contempt and we, as people born free, are loaded with chains and reduced to misery. Shall we still delay

Key question
What combination of factors produced the outbreak of revolutions?

Key terms

Customs union
An economic agreement whereby two or more states agree to lower or eliminate taxes on the goods they trade with each other.

Garrison
A body of troops stationed to defend a town or locality.

Key question
How did events in one area of Italy impact on those in others?

claiming our lawful rights? To arms, sons of Sicily; our united force will be invincible …

The notice went on to explain that weapons would be handed out to those who came to the main public square at dawn three days later. The authorities could not really believe that a revolution was being announced in advance, but they took no chances and arrested a few likely suspects.

On the day announced, the streets were full of people, but whether they were ordinary sightseers or revolutionaries is impossible to say. After what arms were available had been handed out there were clashes with the government troops. Next day peasants from outside the city arrived to join in the rising. The Neapolitan army retaliated by shelling the city, and they were joined two days later by 5000 reinforcements. They found that the revolutionaries had successfully taken over the city and were demanding a restoration of the famous 1812 constitution that had been abolished by the King of Naples in 1816 (see page 12). A compromise was offered. It was refused.

Fighting continued and by April the revolutionaries had taken over most of the island. A provisional government was set up with the help of middle-class moderates, who were becoming anxious about what the peasants might do next. A civic guard was formed to control 'the masses' who were marching on towns and villages, destroying property, freeing prisoners and burning tax-collection records. A parliament was elected and it declared that Naples and Sicily were finally totally separated and divided, and that the King of Naples was no longer King of Sicily. The Sicilians' aim was as always, in 1848 as in 1820, to free themselves from Naples. They were not concerned with national unity – quite the opposite. Theirs was a separatist movement with the aim of breaking away from Naples and making Sicily independent.

Failure in Naples and Sicily
On the mainland, the revolution spread to Naples within a few days of the uprising in Palermo. A huge demonstration demanded a constitution. The king agreed to a two-chamber parliament with limited powers. He also agreed to form a national guard and to free the press from censorship. Nevertheless, peasant grievances over their right to use common land led to fighting in which Ferdinand's troops were successful.

By September 1848 the government in Naples was able to send troops to retake Sicily. The Sicilians were defeated, after an intense bombardment of local towns which earned Ferdinand the nickname 'King Bomba', and by the spring of 1849 were forced to accept reunification with Naples. There the king had already gone back on his earlier promises, abolished parliament and replaced it with absolute rule and a police state.

Success in central and northern Italy

In the rest of Italy other serious disturbances were occurring in 1848. As a result the Grand Duke of Tuscany and the King of Piedmont promised to grant constitutions. Their example was soon followed by the Pope in the Papal States, but in Modena and Parma the rulers had to leave their states and flee for their lives.

Trouble also started in Milan, in Austrian-controlled Lombardy. It began as a tobacco boycott. Tobacco was an Austrian state monopoly and the people of Milan believed that if they stopped smoking then Austrian finances would be seriously affected. The sight of Austrian soldiers smoking in public was an excuse for attacking them and small-scale fights quickly turned into larger riots and eventually into a full-scale revolution known as 'The Five Days' (17–22 March). The commander-in-chief of the Austrian forces in Italy, the 81-year-old General Radetzky (remembered now for the march tune bearing his name) decided to withdraw from the city, not because he was defeated, but because the situation in Austria had changed dramatically. Revolution had broken out in Vienna and Metternich had resigned.

The provisional government set up in Milan by the revolutionaries prepared to continue the fight against Austria. They decided to ask for help from the neighbouring state of Piedmont, whose king, Charles Albert, had just granted a constitution to his people. A week later, Charles Albert agreed to declare war on Austria and the provisional government in Milan issued an emotional and inaccurate appeal to their fellow citizens:

> We have conquered. We have compelled the enemy to fly, oppressed as much by his own shame as our valour; but scattered in our fields, wandering like wild beasts, united in bands of plunderers, he prolonged for us the horrors of war without affording any of its sublime emotions. This makes it easy to understand that the arms we have taken up, and still hold, can never be laid down as long as one of his band shall be hid under cover of the Alps. We have sworn, we swear it again, with the generous Prince who flies to associate himself with our glory – all Italy swears it and so it shall be.
>
> To arms then, to arms, to secure the fruits of our glorious revolution – to fight the last battle of independence and the Italian Union.

In the other Austrian-controlled state, Venetia, a small-scale revolt persuaded the Austrians to surrender, and the Independent Venetian Republic of St Mark was proclaimed in March 1849. Its rapidly elected assembly voted for union with Piedmont.

The impact of the Pope

At first all went well with Charles Albert. His army defeated the Austrians at the end of May 1848, but in the Papal States things were not going so well. The Pope's army commander had disobeyed orders and set off with his troops to join Charles

Key date

The fall of Metternich: 13 March 1848

Revolutions in Italy
1820–49.

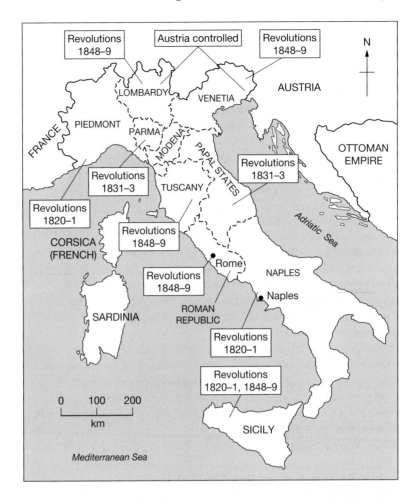

Albert's army. This made difficulties for the Pope, who was not at war with Austria. He decided to keep out of the war and, to make his position clear, issued an allocution, an official policy speech made to senior clerics:

> Seeing that some at present desire that We too, along with the other Princes of Italy and their subjects, should engage in war against the Austrians, We have thought it suitable to proclaim clearly and openly in this our solemn Assembly, that such a measure is altogether alien from our counsels … We cannot refrain from dissociating ourselves from the treacherous advice published in journals, and in various works, of those who want the Roman Pontiff [the Pope] to be the head of and to preside over some sort of novel Republic of the whole Italian people. On this occasion we do urgently warn the Italian people to have no part in these proposals, which would be ruinous to Italy, but live in loyalty to their sovereigns whose goodwill they have already experienced, and never to let themselves be torn away …

Pius IX made it clear not only that he would not join in the war against Austria, but also that he was no longer interested in the idea of becoming head of an Italian federation of states, or even in the idea of the Church lending support for a united Italy. Two years earlier the Pope had 'blessed "Italy"'. He now withdrew his blessing. The Church had turned its back on liberalism and gone over to the side of reaction and absolutism.

For Charles Albert and other loyal Catholics the loss of papal support for their cause was a bitter blow. They would have to choose between following their political principles and obeying their spiritual leader. It was a difficult decision but many decided in favour of their political principles. As a result the liberal and nationalist movements became noticeably **anticlerical**.

Anticlerical
Unsympathetic or hostile to the Church and its clergy.

Armistice
A truce, or ceasefire.

Key terms

Revolutionary setbacks

In June 1848 Radetzky arrived back from Austria with reinforcements and in July Charles Albert's army was defeated by the Austrians at Custoza. An **armistice** was signed and Piedmont withdrew from Lombardy, leaving it in Austrian hands. The Venetians hurriedly cancelled their recently completed union with Piedmont, re-established the former Republic of St Mark and prepared to continue the war with Austria.

At this moment Mazzini arrived back in Italy after long years of exile. The 'war of the princes' against Austria had failed; now it was time for the 'war of the people'.

Charles Albert defeated by Austria at the battle of Custoza: 24 July 1848

Key date

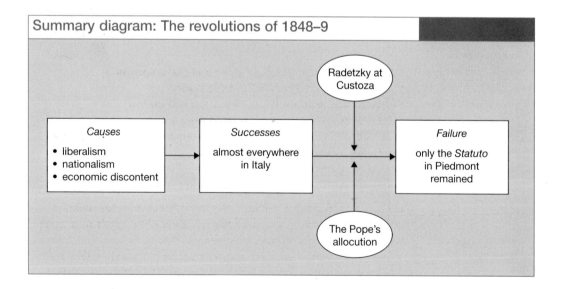

Summary diagram: The revolutions of 1848–9

8 | The Roman Republic and the Revolutions of 1848–9

Key question
What did the Roman Republic achieve?

The Pope flees

In Rome the Pope's unpopular chief minister, Count Pellegrino Rossi, was murdered at the end of November 1848. Rioting followed and the Pope fled from a city in turmoil to take refuge in Naples, while the government that he had left behind announced a series of reforms. It abolished the unpopular tax on grinding corn, provided public building work for the unemployed and proposed the holding of a **Constituente**. The election of these representatives was organised by a special Council of State whose members were chosen by the government of Rome, and the *Constituente* met for the first time in February 1849. Among its members was Garibaldi. Four days later the *Constituente* proclaimed an end to the temporal power of the Pope and the establishment of the Roman Republic.

Key date
The founding of the Roman Republic: February 1849

Key terms
Constituente
A meeting in Rome of representatives from all over Italy.

Triumvirate
A governing group of three men.

Mazzini's Roman Republic

In March Mazzini arrived in Rome and was elected as head of a **triumvirate** (see the illustration on page 38) that would rule the city. In fact, though, Mazzini did most of the work and made most of the decisions himself.

During the 100 days of his power, Mazzini had to deal with a difficult situation, especially as the rich had fled the city, unemployment had risen and his enemies outside Rome were spreading rumours that he was being wantonly cruel and burning people alive. But he governed in a fair, tolerant and enlightened way:

- he abolished the death penalty and the Inquisition
- taxation was reformed to aid the poor
- the clerical monopoly on education was ended
- a dozen new newspapers started up
- he declared Catholicism to be the official religion of the new republic, as a majority of its inhabitants wanted
- he also urged that Rome, Piedmont, Florence and Venice should work together to end Austrian rule in Italy.

Mazzini was described by an American observer in Rome as 'a man of genius, an elevated thinker ... the only great Italian ... in action as decisive and full of resource as Caesar'.

The republic did not last long enough for the real effects of his actions to become clear, but many Romans took inspiration from these months and remembered them for a long time to come.

The fall of the republic

The Pope appealed to France, Spain and Naples to help free Rome 'from the enemies of our most holy religion and civil society', and an army of about 20,000 men was sent from France to destroy the Roman Republic. This they did, for although the gallant defence of the city by Garibaldi became one of the legends of the *Risorgimento*, the odds against him were too great

Key date
The ending of the Roman Republic: June 1849

Lithograph of Mazzini with the other two triumvirs of the Roman Republic, Carlo Armellini and Aurelio Saffi. Mazzini did indeed stand head and shoulders above members of the triumvirate.

and the city fell to the French at the end of June 1849. A French garrison with the duty of safeguarding the Pope remained in Rome until 1870.

Mazzini explained why the Roman Republic fought so fiercely:

To the many other causes which decided us to resist, there was one closely bound up with the aim of my whole life – the foundation of a national unity. Rome was the natural centre of that unity and it was important to attract the eyes and reverence of my countrymen towards her … It was essential to redeem Rome; to place her once again at the summit so that Italians might again learn to regard her as the temple of their common country …

After the fall of the city he appealed to citizens:

Romans, your city has been overcome by brute force, but your rights are neither lessened nor changed. By all you hold sacred, citizens, keep yourselves uncontaminated. Organise peaceful demonstrations … In the streets, in the theatres, in every place of meeting let the same cries be heard. Thousands cannot be imprisoned. Men cannot be compelled to degrade themselves.

Revolutionary defeats

The Pope returned to Rome in the afternoon of 12 April 1850 and was cheered through the streets by the same citizens who had cheered for Mazzini, Garibaldi and the Roman Republic a year earlier, evidence perhaps that even the return of the Pope was preferable to the hardships they had endured over the past months under French military occupation. Yet with the Pope also

Key question
Why did revolutions continue to fail in 1848–9?

came the return of the repressive apparatus of papal rule: the Inquisition, corruption, public floggings and the guillotine.

Failure elsewhere
The Venetian Republic

The Roman Republic was not alone. There was another, the Venetian Republic, that had held out courageously against a siege by the Austrian navy in the course of which the city was heavily shelled in the early summer of 1849. A severe outbreak of cholera added to the misery of starving Venetians, who were driven by their hunger and disease to surrender to the Austrians in August 1849.

Piedmont

Key date

Charles Albert defeated at the battle of Novara: 23 March 1849

Earlier in the year Charles Albert, having apparently recovered from the horrors of his defeat at Custoza and his distress at abandoning Lombardy to the Austrians, decided in March to re-enter the war. (See pages 51–5 for more details of Charles Albert's rule in Piedmont.) Exactly why he made this decision is not clear. Some historians believe that he wanted revenge for his earlier defeat, others think that it was because he had had time to regroup his forces and was ready for action. He may also have believed, wrongly, that France would come to his aid if he re-entered the war.

Charles Albert was not to get his revenge. Within a month he was heavily defeated at the battle of Novara. This was the last straw. A broken man, he abdicated in favour of his son, Victor Emmanuel II.

Tuscany

In neighbouring Tuscany the Grand Duke had granted a constitution at the beginning of 1848. When news of the revolution in Vienna and the dismissal of Metternich reached Tuscany, the government decided to send a small army to fight the Austrians. Workers in the cities began to agitate about pay and conditions and middle-class radical extremists began to preach republicanism. In January 1849 the Grand Duke could stand it no longer and left for Naples, which still possessed an absolute monarchy. In Tuscany a revolutionary provisional government was set up and a **dictator** was appointed in advance of arrangements being made to proclaim a republic. Before this could be done, however, Charles Albert had been defeated at Novara. This left the Austrian army free to sweep down into Tuscany where they crushed the revolution and restored the Grand Duke to his throne.

Much the same happened in Modena and Parma, where the rulers who fled to escape the revolutions were also restored to their thrones by Austrian military might.

Key term

Dictator
Originally a term used in Ancient Rome to denote a chief magistrate with absolute power, appointed in an emergency.

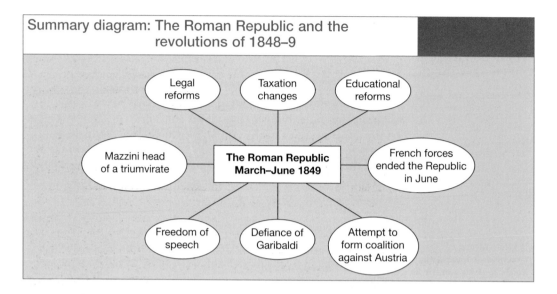

Summary diagram: The Roman Republic and the revolutions of 1848–9

9 | Conclusion

By the middle of 1849 it was clear that the revolutions had failed, just as they had in 1820 and 1831:

- In Sicily, Neapolitan rule had been re-established and the Two Sicilies had been forcibly reunited under an even more absolute and repressive government than before.
- In the Papal States the Roman Republic had been destroyed and the Pope restored to his temporal power by the French soldiers who continued to occupy Rome. All expectations that Pius IX would be a liberal supporter of national unity for Italy were shattered.
- Tuscany, Modena and Parma found themselves again under absolute rule.
- The Venetian Republic came under tighter Austrian control, as did Lombardy.
- Worst of all, the strongest state, Piedmont, had suffered humiliating defeat by the Austrians in two battles.
- The only success for the revolutionaries was that the constitution, the *Statuto*, granted to Piedmont by Charles Albert, survived and would continue to do so, eventually becoming the basis of the constitution of the new united Kingdom of Italy in 1860. But none of the other constitutions wrung from their rulers by the revolutionaries survived.
- None of the rulers forced to escape from their states was away for long.
- None of the states that gained independence – Sicily, Lombardy and Venetia – was able to retain it.

The revolutions had been an almost total failure, and a failure which had involved suffering and death for a very large number of people. As in the earlier revolutions 'Italy' suffered from major drawbacks: a lack of unity, a lack of popular support and a lack of international allies.

Key question
What were the key factors in the failure of Italian nationalism?

Lack of unity

There was a lack of co-operation between the revolutionary groups. Those in Sicily and Naples were particularly at loggerheads. In Piedmont, Charles Albert would not accept volunteers from other states in his army, or work with any other revolutionary groups, unless they first declared their loyalty to the Piedmontese royal family.

The revolutionaries themselves were divided in their aims. Liberals believed that the granting of a constitution by the ruler was the necessary first step everywhere, but the radicals favoured republics. Both groups wanted to expel the foreign occupying power, Austria, but they could agree on little else.

There was no universally acceptable national leader who could co-ordinate policy. Of the three possible candidates, Mazzini, Pope Pius IX and Charles Albert, none was acceptable to everyone. Local revolutionary leaders had no central guidance and the provisional governments that they set up could be any of the following: moderate, extremist, liberal, radical, republican, democratic or monarchist.

Lack of popular support

In the end it was not just that provisional governments and revolutionary movements lacked guidance in 1848–9. They were inexperienced, weak and lacking in resources, particularly military ones. They could not maintain themselves in power having gained it, partly owing to lack of support from the mass of the population, except perhaps while fighting was actually going on. The liberals did not in any case wish to encourage popular support or to involve the peasants. Politics, for them, was a middle-class affair. With few exceptions, peasants found themselves no better off under a liberal-dominated revolutionary government than they had been before. Social reform was not important to liberals and life did not improve for ordinary people.

Lack of international allies

The other vital explanation of revolutionary failure was the military power of Italy's enemies. Austria's military supremacy was probably the single most important factor in the failure of the revolutions. The Austrian armies were superior in numbers, better equipped and much better led than any other army in the peninsula. In any conflict they were bound to win, even if the revolutionary forces had been able to present a united front – which they did not. It was the Austrians who took the leading role in restoring the old regimes in 1849.

In 1848–9 Italian revolutionaries clearly needed allies to counter-balance the might of Austria. But the Pope's influence on the Catholic powers of Europe was clearly **counter-revolutionary**. France, Austria's traditional enemy, might have seemed at one stage a possible ally, but in fact France's only military action – crushing the Roman Republic – was ranged against Italian nationalists. In such a situation, there seemed very little cause for optimism in the nationalist camps.

Key term

Counter-revolutionary
Bringing about a revolution that is opposed to or reverses a former revolution.

A new dawn?

The Italian situation was unexpectedly about to change in the 1850s. In Piedmont the *Statuto* remained in force and gave opportunities for political life to continue in ways that were not possible elsewhere in Italy. Refugees from other states came to Piedmont and settled there, more than 200,000 in Turin and Genoa. They gave Piedmont a cosmopolitan air and a more nationalist flavour which paved the way for what was to come in the person of Count Camillo Benso di Cavour. He was to be one of the great figures in the history of the unification of Italy. But for Italian nationalism to succeed there also had to be changes in European politics, and in particular the emergence of a powerful ally.

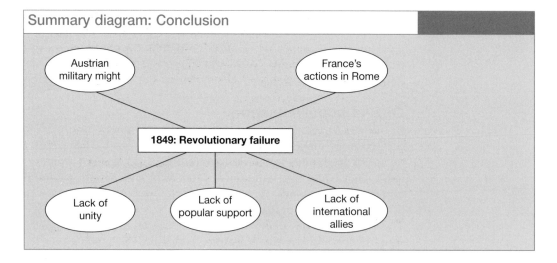

Summary diagram: Conclusion

Study Guide: AS Questions

In the style of AQA

(a) Explain why revolution broke out in Rome in 1848.

(12 marks)

(b) 'The revolutions of 1848–9 in Italy failed through lack of unity.' Explain why you agree or disagree with this view.

(24 marks)

> *Exam tips*
> *The cross-references are intended to take you straight to the material that will help you to answer the questions.*
>
> (a) You should try to provide a variety of reasons to explain the outbreak of the revolution in Rome. Think in terms of both long- and short-term factors. Long-term factors might include: the legacy of the events of the 1820s (page 24); the impact of the ideas of Mazzini (pages 25–9) and Pope Pius IX (pages 30–2); the Pope's reforms of 1848–9; and the activities within the other Italian states at the time.

Short-term factors might include: changes in the Pope's attitude (pages 35–6); the murder of Count Rossi and the Pope's departure (page 37); and the part played by Garibaldi (page 28) and Mazzini.

Try to prioritise and show links between the reasons you have selected. You should provide an overall conclusion and convey some judgement. You might consider whether the influence of the papacy helped or hindered the outbreak of revolution and whether this was a 'copy-cat' revolution or one specific to the Papal States.

(b) This question is asking you to consider different views of why the revolutions of 1848–9 failed. Obviously you will need to focus on the lack of unity, but a well-balanced answer will also require a consideration of other factors. You should try to decide which factor(s) you consider most important and argue accordingly. Your essay should lead to a well-substantiated conclusion.

Re-read page 41. You may be able to add additional categories to those given there. Perhaps your list might include:

- lack of popular support
- lack of international allies
- lack of effective leaders
- lack of military strength
- the power of 'conservative forces' including Austria.

In the style of Edexcel

To what extent did the revolutions of 1848–9 fail in Italy due to poor leadership? (30 marks)

Exam tips

The cross-references are intended to take you straight to the material that will help you to answer the question.

Questions that ask 'to what extent' require you to weigh up one specified cause with others that are not named but with which you should be familiar. Therefore it is worth jotting down on some spare paper a list of the various reasons why the revolutions failed in Italy. These might include:

- Poor leadership. But poor in what sense? Half-hearted, incompetent, or simply divided (see pages 29 and 41)?
- Lack of mass support (see pages 38 and 41).
- The power of Austria and of other states (see pages 37 and 41).
- The attitude of the papacy (see pages 31 and 36).

Each of these might form a paragraph or group of paragraphs. But in which order would you include them? It is best to focus on poor leadership first. After all, this is the issue specified in the question, so it is the one on which you should write most, and if you leave it to the end you might run out of time. Also, only if this issue does not provide a full explanation for the failure of the revolutions are you justified in looking at other possible causes.

The other complicating factor for this essay is that there were, of course, several revolutions in Italy in 1848–9. Did the causes of defeat vary from place to place? If you think they varied significantly, you could divide your answer geographically, looking at the reasons for failure region by region. But even if you arrange the essay in accordance with the different factors you must include examples from the different states.

Do not forget a short conclusion at the end, where you hammer home your viewpoint. Just how important was poor leadership compared with the other factors you've identified and written about?

In the style of OCR

Study the four sources and then answer **both** sub-questions. It is recommended that you spend two-thirds of your time in answering part **(b)**.

(a) Study Sources A and C.
Compare these sources as evidence for the motives and achievements of King Charles Albert. (30 marks)

(b) Study all the sources.
Use your own knowledge to assess how far the sources support the interpretation that the movement for Italian unification was doomed to fail in 1848. (70 marks)

Source A

From: a call to arms by the King of Piedmont issued the day after the Austrians had been expelled from Milan. Charles Albert's Proclamation, 23 March 1848.

Peoples of Lombardy and Venetia, our arms are now coming to offer you in the latter phases of your fight the help which a brother expects from a brother, and a friend from a friend.

We will support your just desires, confident as we are in the help of that God whose helpful hand has wonderfully enabled Italy to rely on her own strength [*Italia fara da sè*].

To show our feelings of Italian brotherhood, we have ordered our troops as they move into Lombardy and Venice to carry the Cross of Savoy, symbol of our royal house, imposed on the tricolour flag of Italy.

Source B

On 29 April 1848 the Pope issued the allocution withdrawing from the war against Austria and condemning popular risings against legitimate rulers. A cartoon from the British magazine Punch *published in May 1848.*

Papal Allocution.—Snuffing out Modern Civilisation.

Source C

From: Carol Pisacane, an early Italian socialist and professional soldier who fought with Italian forces against the Austrians in 1848. He gives an account of war in Lombardy and Venetia in The War in Italy 1848–49, *published in 1850.*

Spurred on by the Lombard aristocracy, Charles Albert declared war on Austria while assuring other countries that he was marching to suppress republicanism. Other Italian rulers, under popular pressure, let themselves be drawn into the war. The king's plan at first seemed about to succeed. Not only Lombardy but even Venetia placed themselves in his hands. Then the outlook changed. When the other Italian rulers saw that the war was just designed to increase the power of Charles Albert, who might threaten their existence, they began deserting the cause. The Piedmontese army was demoralised by inaction and the Austrian forces emerged from Verona. Charles Albert attacked and was defeated.

Source D

From: John Gooch, The Unification of Italy *published in 1986. A modern historian explains some of the reasons for the failure of moves to achieve Italian unification in 1848.*

The failure of 1848 helped to clarify certain facts. Rebellion would not work. Any attempt at progress required united effort if it was to stand a chance of success. Such an effort would fail without a committed leadership which all could accept. Any common political programme must not antagonise those prepared to fight for independence; middle-class nationalists did not want socialism at any price. Also, foreign support was vital if Austrian rule was to end. The diversity of ideas and aims had divided patriots.

Source: adapted from OCR, June 2001

Exam tips

General Introduction: You have 90 minutes to answer both questions, so split your time in proportion to the marks on offer: one-third for **(a)**, two-thirds for **(b)**. You have plenty of time, so read the sources through several times, slowly and carefully. Have several coloured highlighters with you so that you can colour-code sections in each that:

- support or challenge each other as evidence on various points to do with the issue set in question **(a)**
- confirm/disconfirm the interpretation that you have to consider for question **(b)**.

(a) Never paraphrase the two sources. That is not a comparison. Don't discuss each source in order, one at a time. That technique is poor because you will not be giving a good, clear comparison. Instead, pick out individual themes and points and compare what each source says on each one. This approach makes for a genuine comparison and will push up your marks.

These two sources offer very different views of the king's motives and achievements. Both agree that Charles Albert marched to expel Austria from Italy. Against the king's bold claims about liberty in Source A, however, Pisacane in Source C condemns Charles Albert's motives as selfish and his achievements as ineffective. On motives, for example, Pisacane in Source C, argues that the king was concerned primarily with Piedmontese aggrandisement. Source A might support that charge because the king openly admits to using the Cross of Savoy, the badge of Piedmont. Alternatively, the king could be taken at face value by noting that Charles Albert says he has combined the Cross with the Italian tricolour to stress that Piedmont is acting in the name of the Italian brotherhood.

How might such contradictions be explained? If you consider the nature of the two sources, you can compare the view taken by each source on Charles Albert's achievements: an official proclamation (Source A) seeking support across Italy for Charles Albert's actions (Source A) as against the hostile political position of Pisacane (you are told about this directly in the introduction to Source C). The dates help you too: Source A was written in 1848 in an atmosphere of hope as the war was about to start, whereas Pisacane (Source C) wrote after everything had gone wrong and he was looking for the reasons why the revolutions of 1848–9 had failed. Pisacane was bitter.

Always consider the context and provenance of the actual sources you have to use; that information tells you so much and will really push you up the mark bands.

(b) As in **(a)**, don't view the sources one at a time, trawling through each one in turn listing what it says about why the cause of unification failed. Instead, look at them thematically as a set. Thus Sources A and C consider Piedmont's self-interest; Sources B, C and D look at issues of leadership; Sources C and D consider both Italian disunity and Austrian power, and Sources C and D also examine political objectives. If you construct your answer in this way, you will give a real and a full comparison (as required).

Note carefully the instructions in the second sub-question. Each of these areas needs to be judged not against the sources directly, but in the light of the degree to which what you know supports or undermines what the sources say. The question asks you to 'Use your own knowledge to assess how far the sources support the interpretation that …'.

Note the word 'doomed' near the end of the question. For high marks you will need to consider that: not just failure, but doomed to failure. They are not the same thing. Source C says nothing about inevitable failure, whereas Source D implies the revolutions were bound to fail.

Finally, note the date: 1848. The sources talk only of 1848, but you know that that was not the end. Hostilities continued (e.g. the renewal of hostilities by Piedmont in 1849, the continued resistance of the Venetian Republic). Your own knowledge is the means by which the question tells you to judge what the sources say about the cause being doomed to fail in 1848. You know otherwise, so say so (but don't be tempted to go on to talk of eventual unification in 1859–70).

3 Piedmont, Cavour and Italy

POINTS TO CONSIDER

This chapter covers vital material, focusing on the way in which the northern state of Piedmont spearheaded the successful unification of Italy under its prime minister, Count Camillo de Cavour. The main areas to consider are:

- Piedmont and Charles Albert
- Cavour
- The war of 1859
- Cavour and Garibaldi

Try to avoid making final judgements on Garibaldi until you have read the next chapter.

Key dates

1815		Victor Emmanuel I returned to Piedmont as one of the Restored Monarchs
1821		Victor Emmanuel I abdicated
1831		Charles Albert became King of Piedmont
1848	February	Charles Albert issued the *Statuto*
	March 23	Charles Albert declared war on Austria
	July	Charles Albert defeated at Custoza
1849	March	Charles Albert defeated at Novara
		Charles Albert abdicated; succeeded by Victor Emmanuel II
1852		Cavour became prime minister
1854–6		The Crimean War
1858	July	Cavour and Louis Napoleon met at Plombières
1859	April 29	France and Piedmont went to war with Austria
	June 4	The battle of Magenta
	June 24	The battle of Solferino
	July 11	Truce at Villafranca
	July	Cavour resigned
1860	January	Cavour resumed the premiership of Piedmont
		Garibaldi's conquest of southern Italy
1861	March	Victor Emmanuel proclaimed King of Italy
		Death of Cavour

1 | Background History

Key question
Why did Piedmont become so central to the unification process?

In 1720 the Dukes of Savoy, who ruled over the then poor and backward state of Piedmont in north-west Italy, became kings of the island of Sardinia. Piedmont and Sardinia together came to be known as the Kingdom of Sardinia, or Sardinia-Piedmont, but most usually just as Piedmont.

At the end of the eighteenth century Piedmont had only a small population, most of whom were peasants. Although a large number of children were born, the death rate was very high and life expectancy was short. The number of people living in the capital, Turin, was declining, there was little or no industry, and the countryside was poverty stricken.

Nevertheless, Piedmont had two advantages over neighbouring states:

- Unlike the other states it had a very strong army.
- It was well governed by an absolute monarch. The king, as head of state, made all the decisions and all the laws, decided what taxes should be levied and what they should be spent on, and appointed government ministers. He alone could declare war or make peace. There was no parliament and so the people had no share in government, no votes and no say in what happened.

French rule

At the end of the eighteenth century, Piedmont made an alliance with Austria. The Piedmontese royal family was closely connected by marriage with the French royal family and this made them automatically an enemy of the French Republic, which had deposed and executed Louis XVI, and then of Napoleon. In 1792, when the French army attacked Nice and Savoy, to the west of Piedmont, Austria and Piedmont declared war on France.

The war went badly for the allies with the result that, during 1799 and again from 1802 to 1814, Piedmont was united with France. This meant that Piedmont came into very close contact with French law and French government organisation:

- Piedmontese schools became part of the French education system.
- Piedmont's young men were conscripted into the French army.
- French became the language of polite society as well as of government, and the well-to-do members of society became more and more French in outlook.

There was no great opposition to French rule and the middle classes even found it to their advantage as it provided career opportunities. In government service and in the army, they were allowed to fill posts previously reserved only for members of the nobility. Only towards the end of French occupation was there unrest and dissatisfaction, with young men setting up anti-French secret societies.

A period of reaction 1815–31

In 1815 the King of Piedmont, Victor Emmanuel I, who had been in exile in Sardinia during the Napoleonic years, returned to Turin as one of the Restored Monarchs (see page 8). To make himself more welcome he abolished conscription and reduced taxation; but on his ministers' advice he announced that Piedmont was still bound by the laws made before 1800, which many considered out of date, and that these could not now be changed. Piedmont became once again an absolute monarchy. The French legal system, the *Code Napoléon* (see page 5), was abolished along with equal justice for all. Criminal trials were no longer open or fair, the only good thing being that torture was not reintroduced.

In 1819, just as local and central government were being modernised in Piedmont, alarms about the possibility of a revolution led to modernisation being brought to a sudden end. Membership of revolutionary secret societies was growing at this time and some moderate Piedmontese hoped that this would encourage the king to introduce political and other reforms. They were disappointed but not surprised, knowing there was little chance of action by Victor Emmanuel I or his brother and heir **Charles Felix**. They pinned their hopes instead on the second-in-line to the throne, Charles Albert.

On his return to Piedmont from exile in France, where he had lived since his father died when he was only two years old, Charles Albert saw just how severe and oppressive Piedmont's government had become. He showed sympathy with revolutionary students injured in riots in Turin and was known to have connections with revolutionary officers in the army. In March 1821 the liberals appealed to him to lead a revolution. Initially he agreed, but soon he changed his mind

While he was dithering a revolutionary group seized the fortress of Alessandria in Genoa and established a provisional government calling itself the 'Kingdom of Italy' and, rather foolishly, declaring war on Austria.

Abdication

At this stage the 62-year-old Victor Emmanuel, tired of being pressured by revolutionary groups to grant political and social reforms and worried by reports of new army mutinies in Turin, decided to abdicate. He left for Nice, close to the western frontier of Piedmont, as revolution spread throughout his kingdom.

His heir, and younger brother, Charles Felix, was away from Piedmont and so Charles Albert seized the initiative and set up a new government and granted a new constitution. But when Charles Felix denounced him as a usurper, Charles Albert fled and the legitimate monarch gained control of Piedmont with the aid of Austrian forces. He promptly revoked the new constitution. Only in 1831, when Charles Felix died, did Charles Albert become, at last, King of Piedmont.

Key dates

Victor Emmanuel I returned to Piedmont as one of the Restored Monarchs: 1815

Victor Emmanuel I abdicated: 1821

Charles Albert became King of Piedmont: 1831

Key figure

Charles Felix 1798–1849
King of Piedmont from 1821 to 1831, whose undistinguished reign was marked by political repression and economic stagnation.

Key question
How significant a role did Charles Albert play in Italian unification?

Charles Albert
Politics

The new king's earlier career had been marked by contradictions, and the same pattern now reasserted itself, so that it is very difficult for historians to interpret his real aims.

On the one hand, Charles Albert could give the impression of being an old-fashioned ruler, as in the illustration below. It seemed that he would be as absolute and oppressive a monarch as Victor Emmanuel or Charles Felix:

- He began his reign by signing a treaty with Austria and threatening to attack the Liberal government then in power in France.
- He refused to pardon the political prisoners left over from the 1821 revolutions.
- He increased the power of the Church in Piedmont.
- He tightened the already severe censorship laws.

Small wonder, then, that Mazzini and Garibaldi, two key nationalist figures, left Piedmont, soon to be followed by Gioberti (see page 30) who, anxious to publish his proposals for a federation of Italian states presided over by the Pope, left for the liberal city of Brussels. Another figure, Count Camillo de Cavour, also left Piedmont, which he dubbed 'that intellectual hell', preferring the greater freedom of expression found almost anywhere else, even in Austrian Lombardy.

A portrait of Charles Albert as a traditional ruler of the *ancien régime.*

On the other hand, some of Charles Albert's actions were those of a reformer:

- He made helpful changes in trade laws, reducing duties on imported goods and signing trade treaties with other states.
- He tidied up the legal system and its laws.
- He allowed non-nobles to fill senior posts in the army and the royal advisory council.
- Most important of all, in 1848–9 he granted his people a constitution which would survive to become the constitution of the united Italy of the 1860s.

Motives and character

Historians have tried to explain why Charles Albert changed from a liberal to reactionary and back to being a liberal again, but have not found any satisfactory answer. Truly he was, as some contemporaries dubbed him, *Re Tentenua* – 'the wobbling king'.

One suggestion is that he had always been a nationalist, perhaps even a secret revolutionary; and, once king, was only waiting for a suitable opportunity to declare himself. '*Italia fara da se*' ('Italy will make herself by herself') he famously insisted in the 1840s. Perhaps this was his wish all along. Yet this interpretation is not very convincing, since several of his actions after 1831, for instance his alliance with Austria, were reactionary.

Part of the answer must lie in Charles Albert's own complicated character. Many described him as secretive and unsociable, seldom showing any emotion, and some have believed him out of touch with reality. His attraction to the more mystical aspects of Catholicism, and his habit of wearing a **hair shirt**, are not necessarily signs of mental imbalance. But his belief that he was cut out to be a soldier and a leader of men was at best unrealistic. Admittedly he could be energetic and enterprising on occasions, but he lacked sustained determination as well as high-level abilities. Yet Charles Albert took to heart the idea of himself as a military leader and even came to believe, with disastrous results, that he was the military genius who would destroy the Austrian hold on Lombardy and Venetia.

Changing times

To understand fully Charles Albert's actions we also need to be aware of the changing circumstances in which his policies were made. Liberal influences were growing, so that from 1841, for instance, non-political gatherings, such as scientific conferences, were allowed for the first time. Although seemingly non-political, such meetings often helped to spread liberal and nationalist ideas. At one such congress, held in 1846, Charles Albert was referred to as 'the Italian leader who would drive out the foreigners', an idea which gave the king immense satisfaction.

As the 1840s wore on, the pressure for liberal reforms grew. In Turin there were peaceful demands for a constitution from the small but well-educated and outspoken middle and professional social classes. In Genoa, still smarting from the loss of its

Key question
Why is it so hard to fathom Charles Albert's motives?

Hair shirt
A garment made of haircloth, causing discomfort to the body and thereby, according to believers, bringing its wearer closer to God.

Key term

independence (see page 8) and where Mazzini was a major influence, demands were more violent and revolutionary.

1848 and the *Statuto*

The unrest in Turin spread, culminating in October 1847 in noisy demonstrations and threats of revolution which persuaded Charles Albert to agree to reforms and to grant a constitution early in the following year. As a devout Catholic he was probably influenced by the limited reforms recently introduced in the Papal States by Pius IX in his liberal phase (see page 32).

Charles Albert's general reforms were aimed at taking some of the power away from the monarchy and putting it into the hands of government officials. For instance, the police were in future to be under the control of the **Minister of the Interior**. Local government was also re-organised and local councils were elected.

The constitution that the king had promised was issued in the form of 14 articles on 8 February 1848 and was known as the *Statuto*:

> Now, therefore, that the times are ripe for greater things and, in the midst of the changes which have occurred in Italy, we hesitate no longer to give our people the most solemn proof that we are able to give of the faith which we continue to repose in their devotion and discretion …
>
> We have resolved and determined to adopt the following bases of a fundamental statute for the establishment in our states of a complete system of representative Government …
>
> Article 2 The person of the Sovereign is sacred and inviolable. His ministers are responsible.
>
> Article 3 To the King alone belongs the executive power. He is the supreme head of the State. He commands all the forces both naval and military; declares war, concludes treaties of peace, alliance and commerce; nominates to all offices, and gives all the necessary orders for the execution of the laws without suspending or dispensing with the observance thereof …
>
> Article 6 The legislative power will be collectively exercised by the King and the two Chambers.
>
> Article 7 The first of these Chambers will be composed of members nominated by the King for life; the second will be elective, on the basis of the census to be determined.
>
> Article 8 The proposal of laws will appertain to the King and to each of the Chambers but with the distinct understanding that all laws imposing taxes must originate in the elective Chamber …
>
> Article 10 No tax may be imposed or levied if not assented to by the Chambers and sanctioned by the King.
>
> Article 11 The press will be free but subject to restraining laws.
>
> Article 12 Individual liberty will be guaranteed.

The stress on representative government here must have cheered the reformers, but the articles were not very clearly expressed. Perhaps this was intentional, as a way for Charles Albert to avoid giving too much of his power away. Phrases such as

Key question
How liberal was the new constitution?

Key date

Charles Albert issued the *Statuto*: February 1848

Key term

Minister of the Interior
The European equivalent of the British Home Secretary, the minister responsible for, among other things, police and internal security.

'The King's Ministers are responsible' left it uncertain for what or to whom they were responsible – to the king? To the chambers? To the people? Equally unclear is the reference to the 'restraining laws' limiting the freedom of the press. Some form of censorship is implied, but we do not know how moderate or severe it might be.

The full *Statuto* was published in March 1848 and included a number of other clauses relating to legal equality for all, whatever their religion, and for equal employment opportunities. It did not lay down who would elect members of the lower chamber. This was fixed later when the vote was given to men who could read and write and who paid taxes – in fact only about two per cent of the population of Piedmont.

The constitution was not a parliamentary one except in a very limited way, since it allowed the king to keep most of his existing rights. Nevertheless, it was undoubtedly a major advance. Many of Charles Albert's ministers thought it too extreme and so resigned, being replaced by more liberal-minded men.

Piedmont and Italian unification

Meanwhile, events outside Piedmont were moving rapidly and may well have influenced Charles Albert's decision to proclaim the constitution. Revolutions in Sicily, Naples, Lombardy and Venetia broke out in rapid succession between January and March 1848 (see pages 32–4). In Austrian Lombardy, Piedmont's eastern neighbour, extreme revolutionaries wanted an independent republic, while more moderate ones wanted union with Piedmont. Charles Albert saw advantages in putting himself at the head of a Lombard revolt against Austria, as eventually Piedmont might be able to dominate or even annex Lombardy. Typically though he hesitated, undecided whether to take military action or not, afraid that his absence might allow his own revolutionaries to stir up trouble in Genoa, the part of Piedmont most likely to organise a revolution.

Key question
Why did Charles Albert go to war with Austria?

War with Austria

Eventually public pressure and news that the revolutionary government now established in Venetia had voted for union with Piedmont persuaded Charles Albert to declare war on 23 March 1848: 'For the purpose of more fully showing by outward signs the sentiments of Italian unity, we wish that our troops should enter the territory of Lombardy and Venetia, bearing the arms of Savoy [the royal family of Piedmont] above the Italian tri-coloured flag'.

Again historians have argued about Charles Albert's motives. Did he act out of self-interest in the expectation of Lombardy and Venetia being 'fused' with Piedmont as the price of his help, thus merely clothing essentially **imperialistic** aims with appropriately nationalistic language? Or was he genuinely concerned to support a revolt against the foreigner, Austria, and make himself leader of a national independence movement?

Key dates
Charles Albert declared war on Austria: 23 March 1848

Charles Albert defeated at Custoza: July 1848

Key term
Imperialistic
Motivated by the desire to dominate or capture other people's territory.

Key dates

Charles Albert
defeated at Novara:
March 1849

Charles Albert
abdicated; succeeded
by Victor Emmanuel
II: March 1849

The decision to act finally made, Charles Albert entered the war with enthusiasm. His army of 60,000 men, incompetently led by himself and ill-prepared for war, crossed into Lombardy and occupied the capital, Milan. The Austrians, who had already evacuated the city, brought up reinforcements and defeated Charles Albert at Custoza on the border with Venetia. The king had no choice but to ask for an armistice. This allowed the Piedmontese army to withdraw from Lombardy, leaving it again in Austrian hands.

Charles Albert broke the news to his people in a carefully edited version of events:

> The want of provisions forced us to abandon the positions we had conquered ... for even the strength of the brave soldier has its limits. But the throbs of my heart were ever for Italian independence ... Show yourselves strong in a first misfortune ... have confidence in your king. The cause of Italian independence is not yet lost.

Early in 1849, having regrouped his forces and been persuaded, incorrectly, by his chief minister that Louis Napoleon, the newly elected President of the French Republic, would come to his aid if Piedmont again attacked Austria, Charles Albert re-entered the war but with as little success as before. He was heavily defeated by the Austrians at Novara, and then abdicated in favour of his son.

Charles Albert's legacy

Key question
What was the
significance of
Charles Albert's
reign?

The king's unsuccessful attempt to defeat Austria in battle was a major blow for Italian nationalists. Clearly, while Austria remained so powerful there was no way in which Italy could gain independence or unity without outside help. Yet at least this blunt fact was now obvious, and future Italian leaders could learn this lesson.

Charles Albert's other main legacy was the *Statuto*, which outlived him, the one tangible result in Italy of the revolutions of 1848. Victor Emmanuel II, who succeeded his father in March 1849, has traditionally been seen as a courageous figure defying Austrian plans for the *Statuto*'s abolition. Yet most historians now think that Victor Emmanuel was not particularly anxious to keep the constitution but was pressured into doing so by the Austrians themselves, who feared that if he got rid of it he would become so unpopular that not only he, but the monarchy itself, would be threatened. In Austrian eyes anything, even a state with a moderately liberal constitution, was better than a republic.

The constitution therefore remained in force, and in spite of its limitations gave an opportunity for an active political life in Piedmont, something that did not then exist anywhere else in Italy. With a reasonably free press, an elected if unrepresentative assembly, and a certain amount of civil liberty and legal equality, Piedmont attracted refugees from the rest of Italy during the next decade. This was to be a period dominated by the political leadership of Cavour, the military successes of Garibaldi and the interventions of Louis Napoleon of France.

Summary diagram: Piedmont and Charles Albert

2 | Cavour

Cavour as prime minister

Cavour became prime minister with an expert knowledge of economic and financial affairs, and under his guidance Piedmont undoubtedly became a more developed and richer state. Its trade increased in value by 300 per cent in the 1850s, its industries flourished, and its railways became the envy of Italy. By 1860, Piedmont's 800 kilometres of railway track constituted one-third of the peninsula's total.

Yet in 1852 Cavour had only a limited knowledge and understanding of foreign affairs. In the 1830s he had expressed a vague wish that Italy should be united and free from Austrian domination. He hoped, he said, 'for the soonest possible emancipation of Italy from the barbarians who oppress her' but was worried because 'a crisis of at least some violence is inevitable'. He wanted this crisis 'to be as restrained as the state of things allows' because he feared that revolutionary movements, with their stress on republicanism and social upheaval, 'would only make unity more difficult to achieve'. But too much should not be read into these remarks, for in the 1850s he still referred on a number of occasions to the idea of Italian unity as 'rubbish'. Probably he did not begin to see it as a realistic aim until 1859.

The Crimean War

Cavour quickly gained the experience in foreign affairs. Two years after he took office an international crisis led to the start of the **Crimean War**. Traditionally Cavour has been seen as happily joining in the war against Russia in order to gain the friendship of Britain and France and to be sure of some of the spoils, as well as a seat at the eventual peace conference. Undoubtedly this motive did influence his decision to join in the war.

Key question
How important was Cavour in the creation of a united and independent Italy?

Key question
How successful was Cavour in
(a) domestic and
(b) foreign affairs?

Cavour became Prime Minister of Piedmont: 1852

The Crimean War: 1854–6

Key dates

Crimean War
A war fought between Britain and France, with some support from Piedmont, against Russia. Austria decided to remain neutral.

Key term

Profile: Count Camillo Benso di Cavour 1811–61

1811	– Born in Piedmont, the second son of a rich noble, who was a successful businessman and a minister in the government of Victor Emmanuel I
1821	– Sent away to the Royal Military Academy; rebellious student, always in trouble
1820s	– Worked for a short time in the service of Charles Albert, and then became an officer in the army, where again he had a reputation as a rebel. Developed an interest in economics and politics while serving at a frontier post
1833	– Left the army and visited London and Paris. His interest was sparked by Britain's industrial growth, and especially by its industrial cities, railways and banking system
1835	– Returned to Piedmont. He then took over running part of the family estate, importing artificial fertilisers from the USA and making use of new agricultural methods and machinery. He continued his study of economics and politics and began writing articles on a wide range of subjects
1846	– Wrote on his favourite subject, railways, which he described as the great marvel of the nineteenth century. Helped to set up the Bank of Turin, himself becoming one of its first 10 directors
1847	– Charles Albert freed the press from censorship and Cavour founded his own publication, *Il Risorgimento*, and used it to publicise his political ideas. Elected to the first Piedmontese parliament; soon became well known as a non-revolutionary, liberal politician
1850	– Appointed Minister of Agriculture, Commerce and the Navy. He made free trade treaties with France, Britain and Belgium, and even with Austria. Prime Minister Massimo d'Azeglio did not enjoy the everyday business of government and handed over much of it to Cavour
1851	– Became minister of finance, after obtaining better terms for a government loan to build a railway than the government itself had been able to do
1852	– Fell out of sympathy with d'Azeglio's traditionally minded government, and made an alliance with a moderately radical

	party in parliament to form a new centre party. Encouraged to do this by d'Azeglio's decision to reduce the freedom of the press slightly, which Cavour feared might lead to a return to press censorship and absolute government
May	– His position as a minister became too difficult and he resigned from the government. He went abroad, and met the President of the French Republic, Louis Napoleon
November	– Asked by Victor Emmanuel II to form a government on condition he dropped d'Azeglio's controversial **civil marriage** bill, which aroused the opposition of the papacy. Cavour was himself a **secularist**, but reluctantly he accepted. He remained as prime minister, apart from a few months in 1859–60, until his early death
1861	– Died

Civil marriage
Marriage without a church service.

Secularist
One who favours the state over the Church.

Key terms

The nine years of Cavour's premiership were some of the most momentous in the history of Italy. By the time of his death, all of Italy apart from Venetia and Rome had been unified. Controversy centres on how important his role was in this process, and on whether he actually intended that the Italian peninsula, rather than merely northern Italy, should be unified.

Cavour's speech to parliament in 1855 presented his vision of a new Italy whose international reputation would be improved further by sending young men to fight in the war, rather than staying at home and taking part in revolutions, plots and conspiracies which damaged Italy's reputation abroad:

> The sons of Italy can fight with true valour on the field of glory …
> I am sure that the laurels our soldiers will win on the battlefields of
> the east will do more for the future of Italy than all those who have
> thought to revive her with the voice and with the pen … so that she
> can take her rightful place among the Great Powers.

Nevertheless there is evidence that Cavour was doubtful. He was swayed by the king, who was eager to take part in the conflict, and also by Britain and France. These countries put pressure on Cavour partly because they knew that additional, Piedmontese, troops would be useful in the conflict and partly because of a more subtle motive. They wanted Austria, as well as Piedmont, to join the war and they reasoned that, if both these states were on the same side, the Austrians would be reassured that Piedmont would not interfere in Lombardy.

Either way, by joining in the war Cavour did achieve his aim of a seat at the peace conference held in Paris in 1856. There he was able to negotiate on almost equal terms with the Great Powers, and there he also made the further acquaintance of Louis Napoleon, now Emperor Napoleon III. They kept in touch over the next two years until, in July 1858, Cavour was invited to a meeting at Plombières close to the Franco-Swiss border.

The Plombières meeting

This meeting was kept very secret – even the French Foreign Minister was not aware of what was happening. Cavour was equally secretive. He had told only Victor Emmanuel and one other minister about the meeting, which was beginning to look like a conspiracy.

Whose were the proposals discussed at Plombières? Napoleon had issued the invitation and organised the meeting. It might be expected that the meeting's agenda would be his, but there is evidence to suggest that Cavour took with him an outline memorandum that contained proposals very similar to what was finally agreed.

Three days later, on 24 July, Cavour sat down and wrote a very long and detailed letter to Victor Emmanuel giving his version of the discussion:

> As soon as I entered the Emperor's study, he raised the question which was the purpose of my journey. He began by saying that he had decided to support Piedmont with all his power in a war against Austria, provided that the war was undertaken for a non-revolutionary end which could be justified in the eyes of diplomatic circles, and still more in the eyes of French and European public opinion.

Both men were aware that unless the war seemed reasonable to Europe's leaders, Austria might find allies. Certainly Prussia made it clear that it might support her German neighbour, Austria; and even Britain, though generally sympathetic to Italian aspirations, would not support a war of unprovoked aggression. Furthermore, the Powers were fearful that Austrian domination might well be replaced by French control. If this fear proved justified, there might have to be a coalition of Powers to defeat this new Napoleon.

The ideal solution, of course, would be if Austria could be manoeuvred into declaring war. But, failing this, what might be a suitable issue on which France and Piedmont could start the war?

'The search for a plausible excuse presented our main problem', Cavour told his king. He suggested that the Austrian Emperor had broken certain commercial agreements and had extended his territory in Italy further than treaties allowed:

> The Emperor did not like these pretexts. 'Besides', he added, 'inasmuch as French troops are in Rome, I can hardly demand that Austria withdraw hers from Ancona and Bologna'. This was a reasonable objection …

> My position now became embarrassing because I had no other
> precise proposal to make … We set ourselves to discussing
> each state in Italy, seeking grounds for war. It was very hard to find
> any …

Unable to find a suitable excuse for France and Piedmont to make
war on Austria and drive it out of Italy, the two men focused
instead on how a future Austria-free Italy would be organised:

> The valley of the Po [Piedmont], the Romagna, and the Legations
> [parts of the Papal States] would form a kingdom of Upper Italy
> under the House of Savoy [the Piedmontese royal family]. Rome
> and its immediate surroundings would be left to the Pope. The rest
> of the Papal States, together with Tuscany, would form a kingdom
> of central Italy. The Neapolitan frontier would be left unchanged.
> These four Italian states would form a **confederation**, the
> Presidency of which would be given to the Pope to console him for
> losing the best part of his States.

Confederation
A loose alliance of
states.

Key term

Cavour told his king that this arrangement was fully acceptable:
Victor Emmanuel would become 'the legal sovereign of the
richest and most powerful half of Italy, and hence would in
practice dominate the whole peninsula'.

Next, Louis Napoleon and Cavour considered what benefits
France might receive from fighting a war against Austria:

> The Emperor asked me whether Your Majesty would cede Savoy
> and the County of Nice. I answered that Your Majesty believed in
> the principle of nationalities and realised accordingly that Savoy
> ought to be reunited with France; and that consequently you were
> prepared to make this sacrifice, even though it would be extremely
> painful to renounce the country which had been the cradle of your
> family and whose people had given your ancestors so many proofs
> of affection and devotion. The question of Nice was different,
> because the people of Nice, by origin, language and customs were
> closer to Piedmont than to France.

The outcome

Hence a deal was almost struck:

- Napoleon estimated that an army of around 300,000 men
  would be needed to drive Austria out of Italy: he would provide
  200,000 and Piedmont and other Italian states 100,000.
- Italy would become four states, loosely grouped under the Pope
  as a figurehead. (A united Italy, if one were possible, might
  become a threat to France or arouse the suspicions of the other
  Powers. For further consideration of Louis Napoleon's motives,
  see pages 110–13.) Piedmont's power would grow considerably.
- As a reward, France would receive Savoy. Whether Nice would
  also be handed over was at this stage uncertain.
- The diplomatic ground would have to be prepared carefully, so
  that Austria would have no allies. Hence a good excuse for war

would have to be found, although as yet neither Cavour nor Napoleon could devise one.

- A provisional agreement was also reached for a marriage between Victor Emmanuel's daughter, Clothilde, and one of Napoleon's cousins.

The arrangements reached at Plombières were largely incorporated into a secret treaty in January 1859, although some changes were made. In particular, Nice was added to Savoy as Napoleon's proposed reward, and the idea of an Italian confederation headed by the Pope was abandoned. But would these plans ever come to fruition? Could a suitable pretext for war be devised?

Summary diagram: Cavour

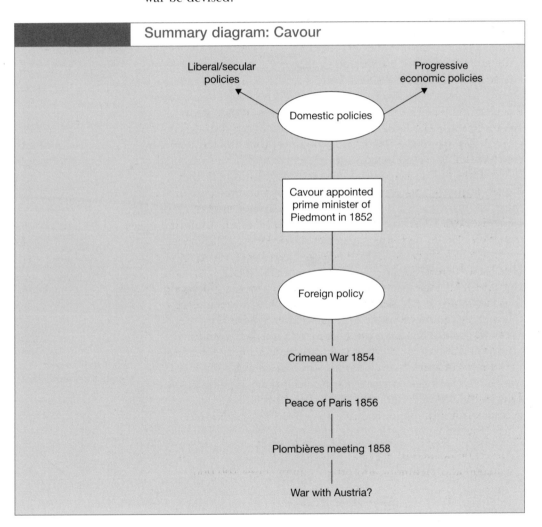

Liberal/secular policies

Progressive economic policies

Domestic policies

Cavour appointed prime minister of Piedmont in 1852

Foreign policy

Crimean War 1854

Peace of Paris 1856

Plombières meeting 1858

War with Austria?

3 | The War of 1859 and its Consequences

Preparations for war

Key question
How did Piedmont prepare for war?

After Plombières and the secret treaty, Cavour began to prepare Italians psychologically for war by writing an emotional anti-Austrian speech for Victor Emmanuel to give at the opening of parliament in January 1859. This included the words, 'We cannot be insensitive to the cry of anguish [*grido di dolore*] that comes to us from many parts of Italy'. '*Grido di dolore*' quickly became a catchphrase throughout Italy to express popular anti-Austrian feelings. Nationalistic feelings were heightened.

Cavour also **mobilised** the Piedmontese army, in March 1859. But without Louis Napoleon's support, he could not risk fighting alone against Austria. There must be no repetition of Piedmont's defeat by Austria at the battle of Custoza, just over a decade earlier.

Yet still war did not begin, and there were signs that Napoleon was beginning to get cold feet. Unless Austria could be made to appear the aggressor, he reasoned, it might be better to abandon the idea of war and turn instead to a **congress** of the Great Powers to settle the Italian question, an idea which displeased Cavour. He feared that Piedmont would not find a place at such a conference and would be considered 'feeble and powerless' by the rest of Italy. But all he could do was express his hope to the French Emperor that Austria 'will before long commit one of those aggressive acts which will justify your armed intervention. I hope so with all my heart'. In other words he was hoping that something would turn up.

Key terms

Mobilised
Organised for a possible war.

Congress
A meeting of several countries to settle key issues.

Declarations of war

Key question
What issue began the war?

In April 1859 something did turn up. Austria issued a demand that Piedmont should demobilise its army. The Austrians themselves had mobilised a large army in northern Italy the previous month, fearing a possible attack, but they could not afford the expense of keeping it at the ready for very long. They dared not disband while Piedmont still had an army ready for war, and so took the dangerous step of sending the ultimatum. Cavour refused to comply and Victor Emmanuel issued a proclamation: 'People of Italy! Austria provokes Piedmont … I fight for the right of the whole nation … I have no other ambition than to be the first soldier of Italian independence'.

Key date
France and Piedmont went to war with Austria: 29 April 1859

Austria replied by declaring war on 29 April 1859. A few days later Napoleon declared support for his ally. The war known to the Italians as 'the Second War of Independence' – the first being that fought against the Austrians in 1849 – had begun. It was a short, violent and terrible conflict.

The battles

Key question
Why did the war end so quickly?

The war started slowly, marked by chaos, confusion and unpreparedness on both sides. Napoleon's troops travelled to Italy by train, as befitted a modern army; but, owing to bad organisation, they arrived in Lombardy before their equipment

Key dates

Battle of Magenta:
4 June 1859

Battle of Solferino:
24 June 1859

Armistice at
Villafranca: 11 July
1859

Key terms

Red Cross
An international
agency founded in
1864 to assist those
who were wounded
or captured in wars.

Ceded
Officially handed
over.

Key question
What were the major
provisions of the
truce?

and provisions. 'We have sent an army of 120,000 men into Italy before we have stocked up supplies', Napoleon complained to Paris. There were not enough tents for the men and, even worse, there was not enough ammunition. The only consolation was that the Austrian and Piedmontese generals were even more incompetent, so that it was some time before fighting could actually begin.

Lombardy was quickly overrun by French and Piedmontese forces. The Austrians were defeated at Magenta on 4 June, by the French army, and at Solferino on 24 June, by a combined French–Piedmontese force. (See the map on page 65.) The carnage at both battles and on both sides was horrific.

The Austrian Emperor, Victor Emmanuel and Napoleon, all present as spectators, were deeply shocked. 'Better to lose a province than undergo such a horrible experience again', mused the young Austrian Emperor, Franz Joseph. Napoleon offered his personal linen to be torn up as bandages for his men, but this gesture hardly compensated the wounded for the fact that the official bandages, along with the medical and other supplies, did not arrive until after the war was over. Hence many who were terribly maimed often lay for hours on the battlefield without any help, until death ended their suffering. The local peasantry stripped the boots from the bodies of dead and dying alike. At Solferino, the French lost almost 12,000 men, the Austrians even more.

The only good thing to come out of this useless slaughter was the arrival on the battlefield of the Swiss journalist Henry Dunant, whose reports of the horrors led eventually to the formation of the **Red Cross** organisation.

The settlement
The war was mercifully short – only seven weeks – because Napoleon suddenly made a truce with Austria. In August he met Franz Joseph at Villafranca and agreed an armistice. He did not consult his Piedmontese allies over the terms. He simply informed King Victor Emmanuel what they were, and the king accepted them without consulting Cavour.

According to the terms of this agreement:

- Piedmont would receive Lombardy, although, to allow Austria to save face, it would first be **ceded** to France and then passed by Napoleon to Victor Emmanuel.
- The previous rulers of Tuscany, Modena and Parma, who had fled when revolts had broken out in their lands, were to be restored to their Duchies. (This was the theory, although it was not clear how it was to be achieved, and it soon became apparent that they would never return.)
- Austria still kept Venetia and therefore remained a powerful influence in Italy.

'The Giant and the Dwarf'. A cartoon from *Punch*, 11 June 1859.

THE GIANT AND THE DWARF.

"BRAVO, MY LITTLE FELLOW! YOU SHALL DO ALL THE FIGHTING, AND WE'LL DIVIDE THE GLORY!"

Napoleon's motives

Why did Napoleon make his sudden and unexpected truce with Austria in July and then, without consulting Cavour, agree to the armistice of Villafranca? There are many possibilities, and the answer probably lies in a combination of them:

- As a military leader, Napoleon had not the stomach for war. The battles of Magenta and Solferino, with their great loss of life, affected him severely. He may well have felt that by bringing the war to an early end he could at least prevent a similar bloodbath.
- The Austrians had been defeated but not routed. Their forces had withdrawn into the stronghold of the '**quadrilateral**'. There was thus little hope that what was left of the French and Piedmontese armies could breach the Austrian defences. Reinforcements would be needed, and obtaining these would take time, and casualties in a further round of fighting would be high.

Quadrilateral
A group of four heavily defended fortresses near the Austrian border (in Mantua, Peschiera, Verona and Legnago).

Key term

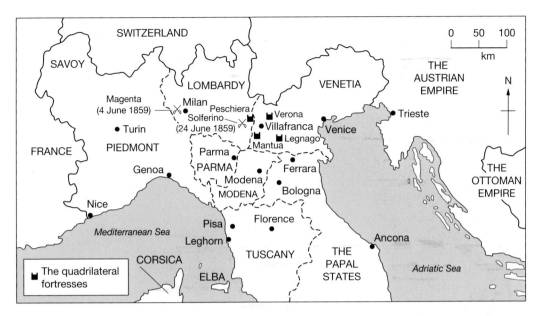

Northern and central Italy 1848–59.

- There was danger too that Prussia, already mobilising along the Rhine frontier, might take advantage of Napoleon's absence to attack France. Alternatively, Prussia might decide to come to the aid of Austria if the war were allowed to continue, and a combined Prusso-Austrian army might prove invincible.
- In France itself, there was growing criticism of the whole Italian adventure (summed up in the cartoon from Britain's *Punch* magazine, on page 64), and Napoleon was becoming increasingly suspicious of Cavour's activities. In Tuscany the Grand Duke had left his Duchy and gone to Vienna, and a provisional government had announced that it wished Tuscany to be united with Piedmont. Revolution had spread to Modena and Parma where Piedmontese armies moved in and took over, setting up provisional governments, while Cavour's agents were known to be encouraging revolution in the Papal States. It seemed to Napoleon that Piedmont was trying to gain more territory and more power than had been agreed at Plombières.

The resignation of Cavour

Napoleon III considered that Piedmont was doing well – indeed too well – out of the war. On the other hand, the French Emperor himself, aware that he had not, as promised at Plombières, driven Austria out of Italy, could not demand Nice and Savoy as his share of the spoils.

Nevertheless, Cavour felt that he had been badly led down. He disliked the fact that Austria still controlled Venetia, and was appalled with the supposed arrangement in Tuscany, Modena and Parma. He was also furious that he had not been consulted over the ending of the war. Generally a calm, reasonable man who knew the importance of compromise, Cavour also had a

Key question
Why did Cavour resign?

Key date
Cavour resigned: July 1859

furious temper. In a hysterical interview with Victor Emmanuel, in which he appeared to lose control of himself, he insisted that Piedmont should continue the war against Austria without French aid. When the king, very sensibly, refused, he resigned as prime minister.

An expanded Piedmont

Cavour was out of office for the next nine months. Yet the situation turned out to be far better for Piedmont that he had imagined. His work as prime minister had borne fruit. Piedmont may not have extended its influence quite as quickly as he had hoped, but the growth in its power was unmistakable:

Key question
How favourable to Piedmont were developments in 1859–60?

Cavour resumed the premiership of Piedmont: January 1860

Key date

- In Tuscany, a carefully rigged assembly voted unanimously in August for **annexation** by Piedmont.
- So too did Modena, Parma and the Romagna in the Papal States. Because of the expected opposition of Napoleon, however, these unions were not immediately put into effect. Instead, provisional, pro-Piedmontese governments were left in control in each of them.
- The Armistice of Villafranca developed into a peace conference held in Zurich in November, and this time Piedmont was invited to send representatives. The Peace of Zurich arranged that Lombardy was to be handed over, first by Austria to France and then by Napoleon to Piedmont. The problems of central Italy were shelved, to be dealt with by one of Napoleon III's favourite methods, a Congress, although objections from the Pope – who feared that he would lose territory in the Papal States – meant that it never took place.

Annexation
The act of taking possession of land and adding it to one's own territory.

Key term

Hence, when Cavour returned as prime minister, he was able to put the final touches to Piedmont's expansion or, from another perspective, to the unification of northern Italy.

Annexation of Tuscany and Emilia ← Modena/Parma/Romagna

In mid-March 1860 in Tuscany the population voted for union with Piedmont. Despite Villafranca, the new state of Emilia (made up of the Duchies of Modena and Parma, together with the Romagna) (see the map on page 125) did the same. This was in fact a foregone conclusion: the war against Austria had whipped up nationalist feelings and the provisional governments had carried out extensive propaganda campaigns:

- In Tuscany, 386,445 voted for annexation, and 14,925 against.
- In Emilia, 427,512 voted for annexation, and 756 voted against.

In Turin decrees were published declaring Tuscany and Emilia part of the Kingdom of Piedmont.

Nice and Savoy

By this time Cavour realised that one way to restore good relations with Napoleon was to arrange for Nice and Savoy to be handed over to him without further delay. A secret treaty between

Victor Emmanuel and Napoleon in March transferred Savoy and Nice to France, subject to the results of a popular vote in both places. These votes were taken in April and again huge majorities voted in favour of union:

- In Savoy, 130,583 were for, with 235 against.
- In Nice, 24,448 were for, with 160 against.

The result in French-speaking Savoy was not unexpected, but in Nice, which was Italian speaking, the vote were suspicious. The presence of a French army in Nice on its way home from Lombardy may have had something to do with it.

Among those who questioned the accuracy of the results was Garibaldi, who had been born in Nice and was one of its elected representatives in the Piedmontese parliament. The transfer of Nice to the French, he later recalled, made him feel 'a foreigner in the land of my birth'. He was preparing a military expedition to prevent Nice being taken over by France when he was diverted by an outbreak of revolution in southern Italy on the island of Sicily.

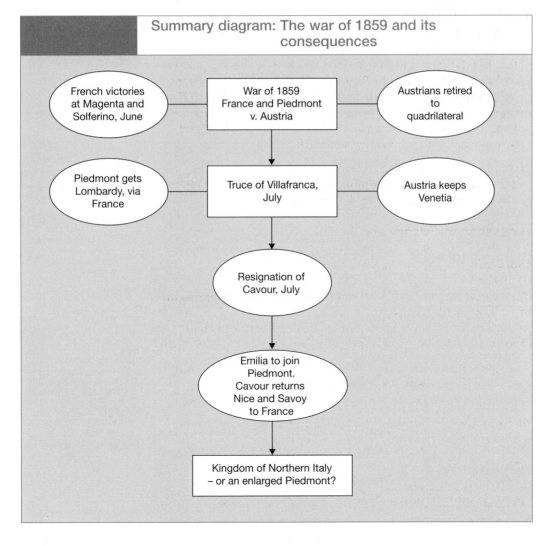

Summary diagram: The war of 1859 and its consequences

French victories at Magenta and Solferino, June — War of 1859 France and Piedmont v. Austria — Austrians retired to quadrilateral

↓

Piedmont gets Lombardy, via France — Truce of Villafranca, July — Austria keeps Venetia

↓

Resignation of Cavour, July

↓

Emilia to join Piedmont. Cavour returns Nice and Savoy to France

↓

Kingdom of Northern Italy – or an enlarged Piedmont?

4 | Cavour and Garibaldi

Key questions
Why did disagreements between Cavour and Garibaldi affect the political/military situation in 1859–60?

How did Cavour and Garibaldi differ in their personalities, aims and tactics?

Historians have argued for a long time about the motives of Cavour and Garibaldi and about the relations between the two men. Their own writings are not much help. Cavour died without writing an autobiography. He did send a large number of letters, but these were 'edited' after his death – with some items being suppressed and others simply invented – to show him in an unrealistically good light. Garibaldi did write memoirs but only covering the period up to 1850, and they are generally unreliable.

Both Cavour and Garibaldi were born in Piedmont, and both played leading roles in the unification of Italy. But there the similarity ends. The two men were highly contrasting figures. Cavour was a nobleman – well-educated, intelligent, outwardly cool, calm and collected – as well as the fat little politician and diplomat. Garibaldi was a rough, ill-educated soldier and leader of men.

Ready to take chances at any time, passionate and charismatic, Garibaldi had ideas that were simple and straightforward, and he did not allow them to get in the way of action. He had come under the influence of Mazzini in 1831 and, although he afterwards abandoned republican ideals, becoming instead a monarchist and following Piedmont's king, Victor Emmanuel II, he always retained his nationalist beliefs and continued to fight for an independent and united Italy. All his actions were aimed at driving out Austria, the foreigner, from Italian soil and establishing an Italian kingdom under the rule of Piedmont. These aims became an obsession which dominated his life and dictated almost his every action.

Cavour was altogether more cautious. He had written in the 1830s about the *possibility* of a united Italy, but even at the time of the Plombières meeting with Napoleon in 1858 he was not fully committed to the idea of a united Italy.

Cavour's tactics

Cavour was realistic enough to know that '*Italia fara da se*' (Italy will make herself by herself), as Charles Albert had hoped (see page 52), was an impossible aim. There was no hope of Piedmont being able to expel Austria from northern Italy without outside help, and the only available source of help was Napoleon and the French army. Cavour had reasoned that France would be prepared to help, at least up to a point, in return for Nice and Savoy, but he also realised that Napoleon would not agree to unlimited expansion of Piedmont and would not wish Piedmont to become the leader of a united Italy. After all, an Italy of separate states could be useful to France in any conflict with Austria, while a truly united Italy might become a possible threat to France herself. It was probably not until Napoleon accepted Piedmont's acquisition of Tuscany and Emilia in early 1860 that Cavour saw greater possibilities.

Even then he does not seem to have been convinced that a totally united Italy was either possible or desirable. Piedmont had gained control over northern Italy by diplomacy and limited war; anything more in the way of territorial gains might involve a disastrous civil war. For him it was time to stop. Not so for Garibaldi.

Garibaldi's boldness

Garibaldi wanted Rome, Venetia, Naples and Sicily, as part of a united Italy, and he wanted them at once. In 1860 he undertook a military expedition to Sicily to unite southern Italy with Piedmont by revolution. His expedition and its results are dealt with in the next chapter (see pages 88–93).

Cavour's motives

It is difficult to know what Cavour thought of Garibaldi's plan. Some historians – especially those who tend to stress the glorious nature of the *Risorgimento* and to see the leading figures as working together to produce unification – believe that Cavour pretended to stop Garibaldi while secretly supporting him. This may have been because he thought of Garibaldi as an ally or because he intended from the start to use Garibaldi for his own purposes.

However, other historians – stressing the unpredictable nature of events and seeing the leading figures as fundamentally opposed – see Cavour as Garibaldi's enemy, opposed to his plans for unification. He pretended to support the expedition to Sicily, partly because he feared that open opposition might lead to a loss of popular support for the government in Piedmont's elections; but secretly he worked to make it fail. These historians believe that he disliked the whole idea of Garibaldi's expedition to attack Sicily and Naples.

'I omitted nothing to persuade Garibaldi to drop his mad scheme', wrote Cavour just before Garibaldi set out for Sicily in April 1860. There is little doubt that Cavour disliked the man, thinking him stupid and probably untrustworthy. Garibaldi had been a republican and had only lately become a royalist. Cavour remained unsure whether this change of heart was genuine. If he were successful in the south, might he demand a republican Italy? If so, this would, he thought, at best lead to a divided country, with a republic in the south and a monarchy in the north.

On 12 July 1860 Cavour complained privately that Garibaldi was 'planning the wildest, not to say absurdest schemes'. But when it became clear, in early August, that the expedition to Sicily had been successful, he changed his tune:

> Garibaldi has done the greatest service that a man can do; he has given the Italians self-confidence; he has proved to Europe that Italians can fight and die in battle to reconquer a fatherland.

At this stage Cavour probably believed that unification was inevitable. He added that 'If, in spite of all our efforts, he should liberate southern Italy as he liberated Sicily, we would have no choice but to go along with him.'

Most historians now favour the interpretation that Italy was unified as a result of the clash of Garibaldi and Cavour, rather than by their working in harmony. Yet the attempt to pluck out the secret motives of historical characters is always hazardous. We are on safer ground in reconstructing what they actually did and in assessing the results of their actions.

Success in southern Italy

When, against all expectations, Garibaldi's expedition to Sicily had proved successful by the end of July, Cavour had to decide how to react. He called for the annexation of Sicily by Piedmont. There were difficulties, however, for while the Sicilians wanted independence from Naples they certainly did not want to replace Naples by Piedmont. Then came news that Garibaldi and his men had crossed to the mainland on 19 August and were marching north towards Naples.

Cavour may have thought that France and perhaps also Austria – both Catholic powers – would intervene if Garibaldi's army proceeded from Naples into the Papal States. France had kept a garrison in Rome since the days of the Roman Republic (see page 38). Any attack on the city therefore would certainly lead to conflict. Cavour was also worried about the growing popularity of Garibaldi not only in Sicily but also in Piedmont and throughout Italy. Might he even lead a revolution and take control in Piedmont, or indeed in the whole of Italy?

Cavour decided that he must act:

- First, he tried to stir up pro-Piedmontese risings in Naples, before Garibaldi entered the city. But these failed, and Garibaldi's army continued its northward progress.
- Cavour then became bolder. He decided to organise an invasion of the Papal States from the north to block Garibaldi's army, which was invading from the south, before it could reach Rome and the Pope.

The invading Piedmontese troops were not well received in the Papal States and met considerable opposition from the civilian population on their way south to stop Garibaldi's army. But Napoleon III agreed to turn a blind eye to the invasion, so long as Rome itself was untouched, and opposition was defeated. As for Garibaldi's forces, they were successful against the Neapolitan forces, winning a victory on 18 September; but their progress further north was barred by a Piedmontese army led by Victor Emmanuel II.

On 26 October Garibaldi and Victor Emmanuel, at the head of their two armies, met at Teano. But there was no showdown. Garibaldi simply agreed to hand over the territories he controlled to the king (see page 92). Almost all of southern and central Italy came under the effective control of the Kingdom of Piedmont. Cavour's gamble on invading the Papal States had paid off, and

Key question
How did Garibaldi's success in southern Italy serve the cause of Victor Emmanuel and Cavour?

made the unification of Italy under the leadership of Piedmont and the government of Victor Emmanuel a reality.

The Kingdom of Italy

Cavour had arranged for the people of Naples and afterwards of Sicily to vote whether or not there should be a united Italy under Victor Emmanuel. Organising the voting was particularly difficult in Sicily where most of population was illiterate and did not understand the Italian of the north. Difficulties were allegedly overcome by providing each voter with two voting slips, one saying 'yes' the other 'no', and by having two ballot boxes similarly marked. Unfortunately even those who could read had no idea who or what Victor Emmanuel was. Even the word 'Italia', which had been Garibaldi's slogan during the fighting, merely confused Sicilians further. Union with Piedmont was not mentioned. Nevertheless, most people probably assumed they were voting for the end of the feudal monarchy of the Bourbons, and there were overwhelming votes in favour of union. In Naples 99.2 per cent voted yes, and in Sicily 99.8 per cent.

Voting also took place in November 1860 in the eastern and central parts of the Papal States occupied by Piedmont, and again enormous numbers voted for union with Piedmont. This time 99.3 per cent were reported to be in favour.

In March 1861 the Kingdom of Italy was proclaimed, with Victor Emmanuel II as King of Italy. Not quite all of the peninsula was now part of the new kingdom: the 'Patrimony of St Peter', the area around Rome, remained under the control of the Pope and in French occupation, and Venetia remained in Austrian hands. Everywhere else unification was complete and under the control of Piedmont.

Cavour did not live to see a fully united and independent Italy. He died in March 1861 from 'a fever'.

Key dates

Victor Emmanuel proclaimed King of Italy: March 1861

Death of Cavour: March 1861

Summary diagram: Cavour and Garibaldi

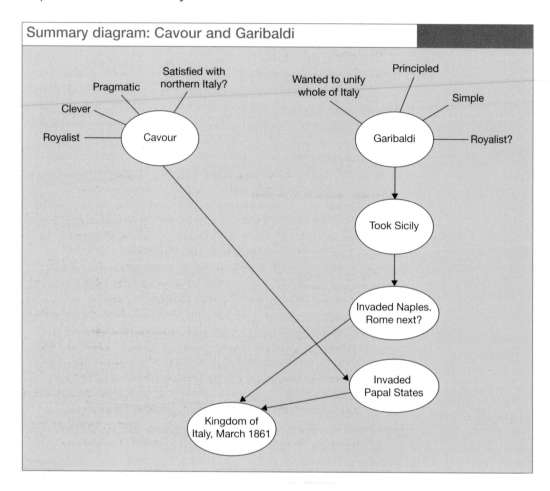

Study Guide: AS Questions

In the style of AQA

(a) Explain why Piedmont went to war against Austria in April 1859. (12 marks)

(b) 'Cavour was only interested in Piedmontese expansion.' Explain why you agree or disagree with this view. (24 marks)

Exam tips

The cross-references are intended to take you straight to the material that will help you to answer the questions.

(a) You should try to provide a variety of factors to explain why Piedmont did this. Think in terms of long- and short-term factors. Long-term factors might include: the dominance of Austria in the Italian peninsula; the desire to avenge the failures of 1848–9 (pages 54–5); the ambitions of Piedmont and of Cavour. Short-term factors would include: the Pact of Plombières in January 1859 (pages 59–61); Austria's demand for the demobilisation of the Piedmontese army; and Cavour's ultimatum (page 62). Remember also that it was actually Austria that declared war on Piedmont, not the other way round.

Try to prioritise and show the links between the factors that you have selected. You should provide an overall conclusion and convey some judgement. You might consider, for example, whether Cavour set out to engineer war or whether he seized the opportunity to advance this cause because of Napoleon III's actions.

(b) This question is asking you to evaluate Cavour's motivation. You should try to think of some examples that could be given in support of the statement and some which would disagree with it. You will then need to decide whether on balance you would agree or disagree and argue accordingly. Don't forget you will need to show material on both sides to provide a balanced answer, but don't be afraid to make a judgement and dismiss the points you find less convincing. In support of the statement you might include:

- Cavour worked to strengthen Piedmont internally.
- He made the Pact of Plombières and went to war to expand Piedmont (his aim was a Kingdom of Upper Italy under the House of Savoy).
- He tried to continue the war against Austria, even after the French made peace.
- Piedmont's superiority bore fruit in 1860 (page 66).
- Cavour was prepared to hand over Nice and Savoy to Napoleon as the price of Piedmontese expansion (pages 66–7).
- He prevented Garibaldi taking Rome (pages 70–1, 91–2 and 143).
- Even the final constitution of the new Italian state might be said to reflect the move begun by Cavour towards Piedmontese expansion (page 127).

In disagreement with the statement you might include:

- In Cavour's earlier career he had talked about a united Italy.
- He may have pretended to stop Garibaldi, but actually secretly encouraged him.
- By 1869 he believed unification was inevitable.
- He reacted to Garibaldi's efforts and brought about the annexation with the south.

In addition you might consider whether Cavour was neither driven by a desire for Piedmontese expansion nor for Italian unification, but other motives, such as personal ambition or love of his monarch. Could it be that he was simply propelled by circumstance?

In the style of Edexcel

How far do you agree that the role played by Cavour primarily accounts for the unification of most of Italian Piedmont in 1861?

(30 marks)

Exam tips

The cross-references are intended to take you straight to the material that will help you to answer the question.

This is a question requiring you to evaluate Cavour's contribution to the unification process by weighing that against other factors which played a part. You only have 40 minutes so it will be important to spend about 5 minutes getting a clear plan and organising your material. Aim to devote about one-third of your time to Cavour's role, and the other two-thirds to assessing the contribution of other key factors that played a part, and reaching an overall conclusion. Above all, resist the temptation to write a narrative of the steps towards unification. What factors apart from Cavour's role will you identify? You will need to be selective in the time available.

Two other key factors you could consider would be:

- Assistance from Napoleon III of France.
- The role of Garibaldi.

Cavour's role:
- Successful diplomacy and co-operation with France (pages 59–60, 66–7 and 70) securing vital assistance against Austria and preventing opposition from Napoleon III to Piedmont's expansion.
- Decisive action in invading the Papal States to halt Garibaldi's advance in 1860, resulting in the fateful meeting at Teano (pages 70–1).

The role of Napoleon III of France:
- Contribution to the defeat of Austria at Magenta and Solferino (page 63), but note the limitations of Napoleon III's support for the expansion of Piedmont's influence (pages 64–5).

The role of Garibaldi:
- His vital contribution in the period May 1860 to March 1861: military success in Sicily and Naples (pages 69–70); his handing over of territories to Victor Emmanuel (pages 70 and 92).

What will you conclude? All three individuals played a significant part and you can show that all three were essential to the achievement of the degree of unification that took place in 1861. Do Cavour's actions link them together? His diplomacy was important in securing French co-operation; his bold decision to invade the Papal States may have prevented foreign intervention (page 70) and it led directly to the creation of the Kingdom of Italy.

In the style of OCR

Study the four sources and then answer **both** sub-questions. It is recommended that you spend two-thirds of your time in answering part **(b)**.

(a) Study Sources B and C.
Compare these sources as evidence for Cavour's qualities as a political leader. (30 marks)

(b) Study all the sources.
Use your own knowledge to assess how far the sources support the interpretation that, in the period 1848–61, Cavour was dedicated to the unification of the whole of Italy. (70 marks)

Source A

From: Cavour, The Risorgimento, March 1848. Cavour, writing as a journalist, describes his reaction to the fall of Metternich and the uprising in Milan, both in March 1848.

The supreme hour for the Piedmontese monarchy has struck; the hour for strong deliberations, the hour on which depends the fates of empires, the fortunes of peoples. In the face of the events in Lombardy and Vienna, hesitation and delays are not possible. We are used to listening to reason rather than the heart, and having considered our every word we must now in conscience declare that there is only one path open for the Nation, for the Government, for the King. War! Immediate war without delays.

Source B

From: Petrucelli della Gattina, writing in 1861. An opposition politician in the Turin parliament assesses Cavour's record shortly before the death of Cavour on 6 June 1862.

Count Cavour's strength does not lie in his principles; for he has none that are inflexible. But he has a clear, precise aim: that of creating a unified and independent Italy. Men, means, circumstances are matters of indifference to him. Cavour possesses overall knowledge of domestic politics; he has grand ideas, at once very liberal and uncomplicated; but he lacks the practical skill of their implementation. This is the vulnerable side of his policy. However, no one questions his superiority in foreign affairs where he is strong and a match for the situation.

Source C

From: Michelangelo Castelli, Count Cavour, *published in 1886. A close life-long friend assesses Cavour's record.*

From the Congress of Paris, Italy gained an unexpected advantage because of his skill. His instinctive understanding of our times made him a believer in political and civil equality. The principles of a free Church in a free State, and that Rome must be the capital of Italy, were proclaimed because he was convinced that they would reconcile religion, the papacy and Italy. It was his habit to proclaim a principle and hold to it. Detailed policy was always governed by circumstances, though he kept his eye fixed constantly on the final goal – the unification of Italy.

Source D

From: H. Hearder, Cavour, *published in 1972. A modern historian assesses Cavour's aims for the various states of the Italian peninsula.*

Throughout his life, Cavour wanted considerable change, though change in the direction rather of Italian independence than unification. Because he wrote in passionate terms of the need to secure Italy's independence from foreign powers – which meant, in effect, from Austria – it has sometimes been assumed that he wanted to create a united nation state. The fact that he did not believe such a development to be remotely possible, until the shattering events of 1860 transformed the situation, should not obscure the sincerity with which he anticipated the independence of all Italian states.

Exam tips

The cross-references are intended to take you straight to the material that will help you to answer the questions.

Read the 'General Introduction' section at the start of the study guide in Chapter 2, page 46.

(a) First read through each extract slowly and jot down points relevant to the stated issue: 'Cavour's qualities as a political leader'. Then see how far the views in the two sources either agree or disagree, and also add any separate points the two witnesses make.

- They are agreed that Cavour wanted the unification of Italy; the language each uses makes this point forcefully.
- They are also in some agreement in praising Cavour's skills in foreign affairs. Gattina delivers a positive overall judgement, while Castelli implicitly praises his handling of the Congress of Paris (see page 59).
- They also agree that Cavour was to some degree pragmatic, able to react to circumstances. Gattina stresses that though his aim was clear, he was not tied to particular means to achieve it; and Castelli adds that his 'detailed policy was always governed by circumstances'.
- Yet whereas Gattina decides that Cavour has no actual principles, merely liberal ideas which he failed to implement, Castelli clearly thinks that he was a real liberal, one who would stick to his principles.
- Castelli also praises Cavour's domestic policies, particularly his attempt to reconcile Church and state in Italy, while Gattina did not deliver such a positive verdict.

Source B accuses Cavour of being unprincipled, whereas Souce C holds a strongly opposite view. It is also worth pointing out that the sources have different points of view. Gattina, we are told, was an opposition politician, and therefore one likely to make criticisms, while Castelli, as a friend of Cavour, is likely to be biased in his favour. Gattina was writing in the thick of events, as they unfolded, while Castelli's account of Cavour was written a quarter of a century later. How would this time-frame affect their perspectives? Is one more likely to be accurate in his views than the other?

As pointed out in Chapter 2, the way to answer this sort of question properly, and so score high marks, is to pick out individual themes/points and compare what each source says on each, e.g. whether Cavour had political principles, whether he was flexible on the day-to-day political details.

(b) The issue you have to 'assess' (i.e. evaluate, picking out its strengths and weaknesses, and saying to what degree it is in accordance with the facts) is how far what you know fits with what the sources argue on the question of whether Cavour was dedicated to the unification of the whole of Italy from 1848 to

1861. We have already been presented with this idea in Sources B and C, which support it. Neither Gattina nor Castelli, however, actually argues the case or puts forward precise evidence to back it up.

What of the other two sources? In Source A Cavour is calling, in vivid language, for a war against Austria. He also talks about 'the Nation'. But is he calling for a war for the unification of the whole of Italy? A war against Austria would not achieve this, and when Cavour talks about 'the Government' and 'the King' he is clearly referring to Piedmont. He may of course have intended that an expanded Piedmont would eventually draw in all of the peninsula of Italy, but there is no evidence for this in Source A. As for Source D, we are given the view of Harry Hearder that Cavour was dedicated to the independence of Italy from foreign rule, but not to its unification into a single state. According to Hearder, Cavour's aims only expanded to encompass a single state with 'the shattering events of 1860'. But in this extract, there is no evidence for such a view. Clearly we have to call, as the question tells us to, on our 'own knowledge'. What points might be made?

- If Cavour did, in the heady days of the 1848–9 revolutions, want the unification of Italy, he clearly changed his mind a few years later (see page 56).
- As a Piedmontese politician, Cavour was definitely a moderniser. He wanted to develop his state's economy and transport system, and here he achieved much success (see page 58). Of course, he may have done this as a means to achieve Italian unification at a later date, but there is no good evidence for this.
- Yet he clearly wanted to expand Piedmontese rule in northern Italy, and to this end he enlisted the support of the Emperor Napoleon III against Austria. The result was the war against Austria in 1859 and the formation of the Kingdom of Northern Italy by March 1860. Cavour may have seen this as a stepping-stone to full unification, but he gave no sign of this at his famous meeting at Plombières with Napoleon III in July 1858. He was very aware that the creation of a single self-governing Italy would be seen as a threat by the French Emperor. The diplomatic game he was playing, which involved ceding Nice and Savoy to France, seemed to rule out Italian unification in the short term (see pages 59–61).
- Therefore Garibaldi's initiative in the spring of 1860 was absolutely vital. Cavour had not planned or anticipated events, he merely took advantage of them (see pages 68–71).

The context of Metternich's overthrow and the events in Lombardy and Venetia, highlighting the focus on Austria, might be used to show Cavour's interests were limited to Habsburg-controlled lands. This theme is reinforced in Source D that stresses independence from Austria and rejects the idea Cavour was dedicated to unification. Reference to the designs of Cavour as late as March 1860 could be made to provide contextual support for this counter view, as could his suspicions of Garibaldi and the efforts he made to constrain Garibaldi and, equally, Cavour's worries about Rome. Against that, the stress in Source B on Cavour's aims could be considered in the context of events in 1858–60 and the even stronger support for the view in Source C could be judged against the Congress of Paris.

So, how might you conclude? Is it possible to agree with the proposition in the question, that Cavour was dedicated to Italian unification throughout the relevant period? It is just about possible, if we argue that Cavour simply put on a show of disapproving of Garibaldi's exploits in Sicily and Naples (see page 69). But it is much easier to argue that the view is simply incorrect. He may well have been dedicated consistently to the independence of Italy or to the expansion of Piedmont, but not to Italian unification. His aims expanded with the course of events.

4 Garibaldi and Italy

POINTS TO CONSIDER

This chapter focuses on the life and achievements of just one man, the controversial Giuseppe Garibaldi. The material is divided into the following sections:

- Garibaldi's early career 1807–49
- Garibaldi and 'The Thousand'
- Garibaldi and Rome
- Garibaldi: an assessment

Was Garibaldi a brave adventurer and a natural leader of men who led a remarkably colourful life, or was he more: the only true patriot of the *Risorgimento* who devoted his life to the cause of Italian nationhood? The balanced conclusion reached by most historians was that he was a mixture of both. Do you agree? Do not give undue attention to his eccentricities and fitful lifestyle; instead, concentrate on his successes and failures, and estimate his importance to the unification of Italy.

Key dates

1807		Garibaldi was born in Nice
1815		Nice became part of Piedmont
1831		Garibaldi met Mazzini and became a nationalist
1833		Garibaldi was sentenced to death for his part in an unsuccessful revolutionary plot in Piedmont
1848		Garibaldi returned to Italy from South America and became a royalist
1849	July 3	The Roman Republic fell
1859		Garibaldi returned to Piedmont and became a whole-hearted supporter of Victor Emmanuel II
1860	May 11	Garibaldi landed in Sicily
	May	Garibaldi took control of Sicily
	October 26	Garibaldi agreed that Victor Emmanuel should control Naples and Sicily
1862	August	Garibaldi was defeated at Aspromonte
1867	November 3	Garibaldi was defeated at Mentana
1882		Death of Garibaldi, aged 75

1 | Garibaldi's Early Career 1807–49

Key question
What sort of a man was Garibaldi?

Today, in Britain, the name Garibaldi is hardly remembered at all, except perhaps as the name of a currant biscuit; but in Victorian England it was a name to conjure with. He was the swashbuckling adventurer, the national patriot, the leader of men, who had struck a blow for the freedom in Italy.

On a state visit to Britain he was greeted with enormous enthusiasm by the largest crowds seen in London for many a long day, all of whom wanted to touch his hand as he rode in a state procession. During the drive he was greeted with a great deal more applause and excitement than Queen Victoria who accompanied him, very much to her annoyance. Soon afterwards his visit was cut short, almost certainly on royal orders.

Giuseppe Garibaldi's life by any standards was colourful and dramatic. He himself described it as having been tempestuous, made up of unusual amounts of good and evil.

Key dates
Garibaldi was born in Nice: 1807

Nice became part of Piedmont: 1815

Garibaldi met Mazzini and became a nationalist: 1831

Garibaldi sentenced to death for his part in an unsuccessful revolutionary plot in Piedmont: 1833

Early life

Giuseppe Garibaldi was born a French citizen in Nice in 1807, but he was only eight years old when Nice became part of Piedmont after the Congress of Vienna in 1815. In any case, both his parents were Italian and he always thought of himself as Italian. His father was a sailor and despite his family's wishes that he should enter the Church, Garibaldi followed his father and at the age of 15 joined the **merchant navy**. It was as a result of this that a chance encounter in Marseilles in 1831 brought him into contact with Mazzini and altered his life for ever.

Key term
Merchant navy
A country's commercial shipping fleet.

Disciple of Mazzini

Mazzini, the founder of 'Young Italy' (see page 28), believed that Italy should be free, independent and united, with the people having a say in government, and that a republic was more likely than a monarchy to bring this about. Mazzini's greatest gift was probably to inspire revolutionary leaders with nationalist fervour and patriotic enthusiasm, and the greatest of his disciples was Garibaldi.

Garibaldi was quickly converted to the dream of a united Italy, joined the 'Young Italy' movement, and in 1833 became involved in Mazzini's revolutionary plans in Piedmont. The plot, intended to start a mutiny in the army and navy, went wrong, and Garibaldi was among those sentenced to death for their part in it.

South American interlude

Fortunately for Garibaldi, he had already left the country before the trial began and so the sentence could not be carried out. Signing on as second mate, he sailed for South America, where he stayed for a dozen years, settling first in Rio de Janeiro. There he found that a branch of 'Young Italy' was already established. He joined and quickly became involved in revolutionary plans. Planning, though, was not enough for him. He wanted action and for a while he became a pirate preying on the shipping of the

New World, and then he joined a rebel army in Brazil. In between campaigns he found time to fall in love and run away with a fisherman's wife who became his devoted, insanely jealous companion for the next 10 years.

After six years of fighting, Garibaldi retired to Montevideo in Uruguay and the humdrum life of a commercial traveller selling spaghetti. He quickly became bored by this and joined the army defending Uruguay against an Argentinian take-over. He raised an Italian legion of **guerrilla fighters** which fought with much bravery if little skill, and was largely responsible for the final Uruguayan victory.

It was during this time that Garibaldi's **Legion** wore the famous red shirt for the first time. Originally modelled on the South American **poncho**, Garibaldi had seen it being worn by local slaughtermen. It was cheap and easy to make and being red in colour did not show the blood, of either cattle or men. Later, inspired by the uniform of the New York Fire Brigade, Garibaldi introduced sleeves, and then brass buttons, making the whole design much more like that of a shirt. After his return with his legionaries to Italy, the manufacture of these shirts was willingly undertaken by young seamstresses sympathetic to his cause (as shown in the painting below).

Key terms

Guerrilla fighters
Small independent groups, using unorthodox tactics, fighting against regular troops.

Legion
The name taken by Garibaldi's irregular troops. Originally it was a division of 3000–6000 men in the army of Ancient Rome. Individual members were called legionaries.

Poncho
A circular cape-like garment with no sleeves or fastenings, and merely a hole for the head.

'The Seamstresses of the Red Shirts' (1863) by Odoardo Borrani.

Instead of the red shirt, Garibaldi himself sometimes wore a white poncho, a relic of his South American days, and his portraits – including that by Saverio (see below) – show him with a circle-brimmed hat tipped over one eye. His shapeless trousers were homemade by himself, but as he never mastered buttonholes they had to be tied up with laces. He preferred a simple life and ate little. Rather rough in manner, he was generally good humoured, but could be ruthless and determined. His main interests were fighting and women. He 'collected' a large number of women over the years in addition to the three he married.

Scandal and gossip followed him, but could not hide his success as a leader of soldiers or his devotion to the cause of Italian unity.

On his return to Italy in 1848 he was to inspire great devotion from his men, and a near-religious adoration from ordinary people. Street songs, ballads and popular prints of the time show

A portrait of Garibaldi by Altamura Saverio.

A lithograph of Garibaldi from 1850 likening him to Christ.

him as semi-divine: in effect a local patron saint, his portrait was displayed in a place of honour next to that of the Madonna in Italian homes (see the illustration above). His charisma was overwhelming.

Garibaldi and the revolutions of 1848–9

In 1848, hearing rumours of a revolution in Italy, Garibaldi decided to return home, accompanied by 60 of his men and a number of out-of-date weapons. When he arrived in Nice, he immediately offered his military services to Charles Albert, King of Piedmont. This was a surprising thing for him, as a declared republican, to do. Charles Albert must have been surprised also.

Key question
Why did Garibaldi switch from being a republican to a royalist?

Key dates

Garibaldi returned to Italy from South America and became a royalist: 1848

The Roman Republic fell: 3 July 1849

Key term

Garibaldini
The soldiers of Garibaldi, also known as legionaries and Red Shirts.

The king mistrusted the offer and refused to see Garibaldi, sending him instead to the War Minister, who also refused the offer. Nobody, it seemed, trusted or wanted Garibaldi and his red-shirted devoted followers, the *Garibaldini*.

Garibaldi enlisted instead in the army of the revolutionary government of Milan in Lombardy, but before his men could see much action the news came that Charles Albert's Piedmontese army had been defeated at Custoza (see page 36). On hearing this, most of the legionaries deserted, and the few who remained with Garibaldi took action in only a few minor skirmishes. Later, an Austrian general remarked that the one man who could have helped Piedmont win the 1848 war was the one man they turned their backs on.

Why did Garibaldi offer his services to Charles Albert? He seems to have believed that only Charles Albert, as King of Piedmont, had the resources to defeat the Austrians and unite Italy. It was a decision that constituted a turning point in his life, as he abandoned the republican preference he had learnt from Mazzini. 'I was a republican', Garibaldi insisted, 'but when I discovered that Charles Albert had made himself champion of Italy I swore to obey him and faithfully to follow his banner.' Mazzini was hurt at what he saw as a betrayal, and Charles Albert failed at first to welcome his new follower; but Garibaldi, always single-minded in his devotion to the cause of Italian unity, could see no way of achieving it except by attaching himself to Charles Albert and afterwards to his successor.

Key question
Why did the Roman Republic last for such a short time?

The Roman Republic 1849

The Roman Republic was declared in February 1849, after the Pope had refused to make political changes to the government of Rome and was forced to escape from the city to safety in southern Italy (see page 37). The Republic was short lived, surviving for only four months. It was led by a triumvirate headed by Mazzini. Under his influence Rome had never been better governed.

Garibaldi and the legionaries arrived in Rome as the city prepared, in Mazzini's words, 'to resist, resist whatever the cost, in the name of independence, in the name of honour and the right of all states, great or small, weak or strong, to govern themselves'.

Garibaldi appeared a striking figure, patrolling the city defences. According to a Dutch artist who saw him in Rome in 1849:

Garibaldi entered through the gate. It was the first time I had seen the man whose name everyone in Rome knew and in whom many had placed their hopes. Of middle height, well built, broad shouldered, his square chest gives a sense of power – he stood there before us; his blue eyes verging on violet, surveyed in one glance the entire group. Those eyes had something remarkable ... they contrasted curiously with those dark sparkling eyes of his Italian soldiers, and his light chestnut brown hair, which fell loosely over his shoulders, contrasting with their shining black curls. His face was burnt red with the sun and his face covered with freckles.

A heavy moustache and a light blonde beard ending in two points gave a military expression to his face. Most striking was his broad nose which has caused him to be given the name of Leone and indeed made one think of a lion; a resemblance which according to his soldiers was still more conspicuous in a fight when his eyes shot forth flames and his hair waved as a mane upon his head.

He was dressed in a red tunic and on his head was a little black felt, sugar loaf hat, with two black ostrich feathers. In his left hand he had a sabre and a cartridge bag hung from his left shoulder.

The Pope had appealed to Austria and Spain for help, but it was not from these Catholic monarchies – which might have been expected to come to the aid of the Pope – but from the president of another republic, Louis Napoleon of France, that help came. A French army arrived at the gates of Rome, but was driven back. Then, during a temporary truce, French reinforcements arrived. The end came quickly as the defenders, heavily outnumbered, fought bravely but in vain. At the beginning of July the Roman Republic fell to the soldiers of the French Republic.

The march to the coast

On the day before, Garibaldi had made a theatrical entry into Rome's Assembly with a sword so bent and battered from hand-to-hand fighting that it would no longer fit in its scabbard. He announced that further resistance was useless. The Assembly appointed him 'dictator' of Rome to make what arrangements he thought necessary. He outlined possible action to the Assembly:

- to surrender the city (impossible)
- to continue to fight inside the city (suicidal in view of the greatly reinforced French army now numbering 20,000 men, twice the size of the defending army)
- or to withdraw as many men as possible towards Venetia, where the Republic there was still holding out against a besieging Austrian army (the only acceptable option).

Garibaldi appealed to the crowd in the Piazza of St Peter:

Fortune who betrays us today will smile on us tomorrow. I am going out from Rome. Let those who wish to continue the war against the stranger, come with me. I offer neither pay, nor quarters, nor provisions; I offer hunger, thirst, forced marches, battles and death. Let him who loves his country in his heart, and not with his lips only, follow me.

He collected nearly 5000 men, almost all the soldiers who had not been killed in the defence of Rome, and began a forced march towards the Adriatic coast.

This march became one of the epic tales of the *Risorgimento*. Over 800 kilometres of mountainous country, a shortage of food and water, and pursuit by enemy troops all took their toll. Only 1500 men reached the coast. Garibaldi's wife Anita, who had accompanied him everywhere during the past 10 years and often fought alongside him, died on the way and he was unable to stop for long enough to bury her. Many of the *Garibaldini* were killed or captured or deserted to become bandits.

Garibaldi himself escaped to Genoa where he was arrested but later freed on condition that he left Italy at once. His career as a revolutionary soldier-hero seemed to be over, the drama played out, the legend finished as he once again set sail across the Atlantic, this time to North America.

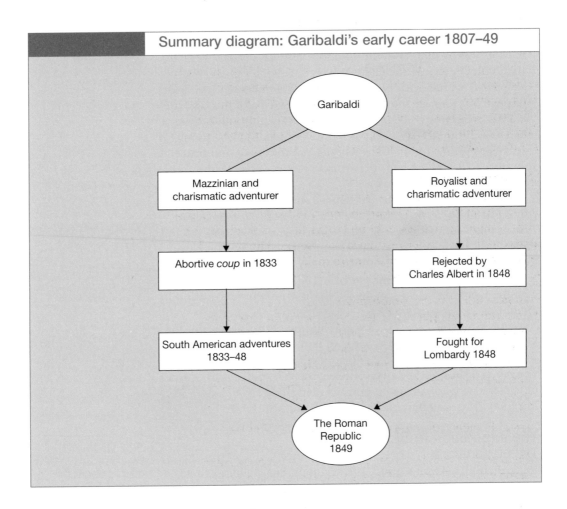

Summary diagram: Garibaldi's early career 1807–49

2 | Garibaldi and 'The Thousand'

Exile and royal service 1849–59

Key question
What caused friction between Cavour and Garibaldi?

Key date
Garibaldi returned to Piedmont and became a whole-hearted supporter of Victor Emmanuel II: 1859

In the United States Garibaldi found what employment he could, eventually going back to sea as master of a ship travelling between the USA and China, until he inherited some money from his brother. He used this to buy half of the small island of Caprera off the coast of the island of Sardinia. There he took up farming but was able to keep in touch with events in Italy through the **National Society**, which was working for the unification of Italy not as a republic but as a monarchy under the leadership of the King of Piedmont.

In the 10 years since Garibaldi had left Italy there had been many changes. The situation in Piedmont itself was greatly altered. Charles Albert had been succeeded by his son, Victor Emmanuel, who was pleasant, easy-going and rather lazy, and not unlike Garibaldi in his down-to-earth honest approach and somewhat uncultivated manners. He was, however, much more politically able than he appeared and managed somehow to keep on good terms with both Cavour and Garibaldi. He inspired great loyalty from the latter, though without returning it.

Cavour was by now chief minister, but his views on the need for Italian unity were still unclear.

After his meeting with Napoleon III at Plombières in July 1858 (see page 59), Cavour sent an invitation to Garibaldi through the National Society to visit Turin. There, at a meeting with Cavour and Victor Emmanuel, Garibaldi was given details of the plans for forcing war on Austria in 1859. He offered to recruit and train volunteers. Clearly, he had thrown in his lot with the Piedmontese king.

In the spring of 1859 the war against Austria began (see pages 62–3 for details of the war). The armies of Piedmont and France were badly organised, but the Austrians even more so, and French and Piedmontese troops were able to conquer Lombardy. Garibaldi's men played an important part in the fighting in northern Italy and Garibaldi was presented by Victor Emmanuel with the Gold Medal for valour, the highest military decoration in Piedmont.

Victor Emmanuel was now king of all northern Italy except for Venetia. But as part of the agreement with Napoleon for French support during the war, Nice and Savoy had to be ceded to France; and the handing over of Nice, the city of his birth, was a bitter blow to Garibaldi, who now decided that Cavour was 'a low intriguer'. A crisis point had been reached.

The expedition to Sicily
The preparations

In April 1860 a revolt started in Palermo in Sicily against the King of Naples. It was almost certainly organised by followers of Mazzini, who urged Garibaldi to take his men to the island, and it was supported by the National Society with its contacts throughout Italy. At the time Garibaldi was working on an armed expedition to recover Nice from France. This would include blowing up the ballot boxes to be used by those voting on whether Nice should remain Italian or again become French. He was, fortunately for the cause of Italian unity, diverted from this plan by news of the revolt in Sicily.

Garibaldi began to collect more volunteers and by early May 1860 had a force of about 1200, mostly very young men, who were known as 'The Thousand'. He also had with him his current mistress and a thousand rifles, but no ammunition, aboard two

National Society
A body set up in 1856 by moderate republicans, aiming to bridge the gap between Mazzini and Garibaldi. Led by the Venetian Daniele Manin, it began to look to the Piedmontese monarchy to spearhead unification.

Key question
Why did Cavour have doubts about this expedition?

old paddle steamers in the port of Genoa, ready to sail in the name of 'Italy and Victor Emmanuel'.

Cavour's attitude

Common sense suggested to the Piedmontese prime minister, Count Cavour, that the expedition was unlikely to succeed. It had been put together too quickly, the number of men was too small and their resources too poor, while it was known that the enemy forces were large. It was also known that previous expeditions of this kind had failed, including a much larger one in 1857. Garibaldi might be a brilliant leader of men but he had no understanding of military tactics. Cavour therefore was far from convinced that the expedition would succeed. Nor was he sure it was a good idea. In his opinion Sicily, like the rest of the south, was too poor and backward to be ready for a take-over by Piedmont. He therefore refused Garibaldi's request for arms and equipment for the expedition, and made it clear that it went without Piedmontese official support.

Some later reports suggested that Cavour tried to persuade Victor Emmanuel to arrest Garibaldi. But it was too late. The expedition had sailed on 5 May.

In a note to his confidential agent in Paris, Cavour made it clear that he had 'made every effort to persuade Garibaldi to drop his mad scheme', but could 'not stop him going, for force would have been necessary', which would have led to 'immense unpopularity had Garibaldi been prevented'. In the end he comforted himself with the idea that if the expedition failed he would be rid of Garibaldi, 'a troublesome fellow', and if it succeeded 'Italy would get some benefit from it'.

Success in Sicily

Garibaldi reached Marsala in Sicily on 11 May. He was lucky to be allowed to land. His two steamers arrived alongside a detachment of Britain's navy, and the local commander – quite wrongly – thought Garibaldi was under British protection and so refrained from attacking, whereas in reality there was no connection at all. Garibaldi benefited from this happy accident. One of his men was wounded in the shoulder, and one dog in the leg. It was an auspicious start.

From Marsala, the Red Shirts advanced on Palermo, the island capital, gathering support on the way and defeating a Neapolitan army in hand-to-hand fighting. In pouring rain 'The Thousand' – now numbering nearer 3000 – reached Palermo at the end of May and found 20,000 enemy troops waiting for them. One of 'The Thousand' described the battle for Palermo:

> There was no sign of any local uprising until quite late in the day. We were on our own, 800 of us at most, spread out over an area as large as Milan. It was impossible to expect any planning let alone any orders, but somehow we managed to take the city against 25,000 well-armed and well-mounted regular soldiers.

Key question
How was Garibaldi able to conquer Sicily?

Key date
Garibaldi landed in Sicily: 11 May 1860

> We were real ragamuffins … we ran in ones and twos through
> alleys and squares chasing Neapolitans and trying to stir up the
> Palmeritans. The Neapolitans were too busy running away
> and the Palmeritans in taking refuge from the gunfire … when
> Palermo finally fell it was all our doing, ours alone. Garibaldi
> showed the height of courage and we too were heroes just
> because we believed in what was impossible.

Garibaldi quickly took possession of Palermo, the garrison
withdrew to Naples and the island of Sicily was his. His success
outside Palermo was helped by the fact that an earlier revolt had
left much of the island in a state of chaos, with bands of peasants
roaming about looking for revenge against Neapolitan troops and
oppressive landlords. Therefore, the speed of Garibaldi's success
was partly due to his dashing and bold style of leadership and
partly due to the caution of Neapolitan officers worried about
possible ambushes of their men by Sicilian bandits and
dispossessed peasants.

Key date
Garibaldi took control
of Sicily: May 1860

Governing Sicily

Garibaldi appointed himself as 'dictator' of Sicily and at first was
sympathetic to the aims of the peasant revolt. He abolished the
tax collected on corn being milled into flour, which was a
standing grievance of the peasants, and won their support by
promising a redistribution of land. Soon, however, he changed
sides and suppressed a number of new peasant revolts. Through
this he lost the support of the peasants but won that of the
landlords whose help he needed to restore law and order. He
needed peace and stability in the island in order to be able to use
Sicily as a jumping-off ground for an attack on the mainland of
Italy and the next stage of unification. His obsession with a united
Italy had led him to betray Mazzini's teaching about the
importance of supporting the underprivileged.

Key question
Did Garibaldi govern
Sicily effectively?

A report to Cavour on the situation in Sicily in June 1860
showed all was not well:

> Garibaldi is greatly beloved. But no one believes him capable of
> running a government … No one wishes to wound him, but all are
> determined not to tolerate a government which is no government
> … He is troubled, irritated and weary beyond belief and his
> conversation clearly shows that the cares of government are
> crushing and overwhelming him.

As part of his law-and-order campaign Garibaldi introduced
Piedmontese laws into Sicily as a preparation for annexation by
Piedmont, but for the moment he refused to hand over Sicily to
Victor Emmanuel. He was afraid that if he did so Cavour would
stop him using Sicily as a base for the campaign against Naples.
Cavour was undoubtedly surprised at Garibaldi's success in Sicily
and probably displeased at the public acclaim. Garibaldi was too
much in the limelight and likely to take too much of the credit for
himself for uniting Italy if he was allowed to continue unchecked.

Cavour would have preferred things done more quietly, more constitutionally and with the credit going to Piedmont, Victor Emmanuel and himself.

Naples

Key question
Why did Garibaldi have such easy success in Naples?

Cavour was correct in his assumption that Garibaldi would next attempt to take Naples and then move northwards. But what could he do to prevent him? He tried to arrange a revolution in Naples in favour of Victor Emmanuel, but this failed. Then he gave orders to stop Garibaldi and his men from crossing the Straits of Messina to the mainland, but Garibaldi was too quick for him: dodging the ships sent to stop him he ferried his men across the Straits to Calabria on 22 August.

Then, although heavily outnumbered, Garibaldi fought his way north towards the city of Naples. When he heard that the King of Naples had left the city, he accepted its surrender, arriving there in advance of his troops, by train and almost alone in early September.

For the next two months Garibaldi ruled as 'dictator' over the Kingdom of Naples, unable to advance any further because the way was barred by a Neapolitan military stronghold in the north.

Nevertheless Garibaldi's plan was, as soon as possible, to move northwards, to the Papal States and then to Rome, and so complete the geographical unification of Italy. The fact that he was delayed in Naples gave Cavour time to act.

Cavour forestalls Garibaldi

Key question
Why did Cavour feel that he had to check Garibaldi's progress?

As we have seen (on pages 68–70), historians are uncertain about Cavour's precise motives at this stage. But he clearly did not much like what Garibaldi had been doing in Sicily and Naples and feared that an attack on Rome, such as Garibaldi intended, would lead to difficulties, especially with France. Napoleon III was already upset because, two months earlier on his way south, Garibaldi had landed a small force in the Papal States. That expedition fizzled out, but the warning of more to come was clear. The danger was that France and the rest of Catholic Europe would act if the Pope or the city of Rome were threatened.

Cavour was aware that many of the men who had joined Garibaldi (the *Garibaldini* now numbered about 60,000 men) were Mazzinians. This meant that they were opposed to the Church and its teachings and would be only too glad to join in an attack on Rome. They were also republicans and this posed another threat. If they won control, the whole nationalist leadership might slip away from Piedmont and Victor Emmanuel, and become again republican and revolutionary. Cavour and Victor Emmanuel must have had some doubt about whether even Garibaldi could maintain control over such a large army of irregular soldiers and enforce on them obedience to the cause he said he was supporting, that of 'Italy and Victor Emmanuel'. It was all becoming very difficult for Cavour.

Cavour's most pressing need was to stop Garibaldi from attacking Rome. The only way to do this was to send an army from Piedmont through the Papal States to meet him before he could reach the city of Rome. The Pope had no wish to see either the *Garibaldini* or official Piedmontese troops in his territory, but Cavour acted anyway. Using the excuse that the Pope was unable to deal with a threatened revolt in his territory, the Piedmontese army with Victor Emmanuel at its head marched through the Papal States. They defeated a papal army on the way, and any civilians resisting the invasion were shot as traitors to the cause of a united Italy.

Unification almost complete

In October the Piedmontese army reached Neapolitan territory and Garibaldi and Victor Emmanuel met on 26 October in what might have been a highly tense scene. But Garibaldi had no intention of doing other than prove himself a loyal subject. With a flourish of his broad-brimmed hat he saluted Victor Emmanuel as 'the first King of Italy' and agreed that the territory he had taken should be handed over to the king.

In the ballots that were soon held in Sicily, Naples, Umbria and the Papal Marches there was an overwhelming wish for annexation by Piedmont. Nationalist feelings were running high after all the drama of the summer, and there seemed no real alternative now that the previous rulers were no longer in place (see also page 71).

On 7 November Victor Emmanuel and Garibaldi rode together in a triumphal state entry into Naples. One of the staff from the French embassy in Piedmont wrote that

> the immense popularity which Victor Emmanuel enjoys in the old provinces of Piedmont owes more to the royalist feelings of the people than to the personal qualities of the King. Events and above all the genius of his Prime Minister [Cavour] have raised him to the position he now occupies in Italy and in Europe. If ever his name becomes famous in history, his only glory will have been 'to have allowed Italy to create herself'. Like all mediocre men Victor Emmanuel is jealous and quick to take offence. He will find it difficult to forget the manner of his triumphal entry into Naples, when, seated in Garibaldi's carriage – Garibaldi in a red shirt – he was presented to his people by the most powerful of his subjects.
>
> People are mistaken in crediting Victor Emmanuel with a liking for Garibaldi. As soldiers they probably have points of contact in their characters and tastes, which have allowed them to understand each other at times, but the hero's familiarity is very displeasing to the King. After all, what sovereign placed in the same situation would not resent the fabulous prestige of Garibaldi's name?

On the day after the state entry into Naples, Garibaldi officially handed over all his conquests to Victor Emmanuel, who in return offered him the rank of Major General, the title of Prince, a large pension and even a castle. Garibaldi refused them all because he felt that the king had behaved badly towards the Red Shirts. He had refused to inspect them and had not signed the proclamation of thanks sent to them. Soon afterwards the *Garibaldini* were disbanded, their services no longer required. As Garibaldi said,

Key question
Why did Cavour and Victor Emmanuel wish Garibaldi to play no further part in Italian affairs?

Key date

Garibaldi agreed that Victor Emmanuel should control Naples and Sicily: 26 October 1860

'They think men are like oranges; you squeeze out the last drop of juice and then you throw away the peel'.

Garibaldi retired to his island of Caprera with a year's supply of macaroni and very little else. Both Victor Emmanuel and Cavour were determined that Garibaldi should leave active political life. As far as they were concerned, his job was done. (As shown in the cartoon below, several key figures wished to snuff out even his reputation.) All Italy except for Rome and Venetia had been united under Victor Emmanuel and the constitution of Piedmont had been extended to the whole of the new Kingdom of Italy. If Garibaldi remained politically active, he was likely to cause trouble.

Garibaldi, however, did not agree that his work was finished. He had his eye fixed firmly on Rome as a future target.

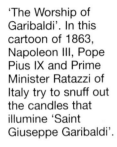

'The Worship of Garibaldi'. In this cartoon of 1863, Napoleon III, Pope Pius IX and Prime Minister Ratazzi of Italy try to snuff out the candles that illumine 'Saint Giuseppe Garibaldi'.

S. GIUSEPPE GARIBALDI

Summary diagram: Garibaldi and 'The Thousand'

Was Garibaldi loyal to Victor Emmanuel II?

1859 – fought for Piedmont against Austria	Yes
March 1800 – Nice (his birthplace) ceded to France	Doubtful
May–July 1800 – took Sicily, which to refused to give to Piedmont	No
October 1800 – handed over Sicily and Naples to Victor Emmanuel	Yes

3 | Garibaldi and Rome

Rome was still occupied by French troops protecting the Pope, but there was continued pressure from Italian nationalists for it to be freed and included in the new Kingdom of Italy as the historical capital.

The first attempt

Garibaldi had always maintained that whenever the government found itself unable to act in the interests of national unity, it was the right of volunteers to take independent action. Thus, in 1862 he returned to Sicily from Caprera and collected together about 3000 volunteers for the conquest of Rome. Apparently with the approval of Victor Emmanuel but not of the Piedmontese government, Garibaldi set off on the march north. He did not know that Cavour's successor as prime minister, Urbano Rattazzi, had planned a similar *coup* to that of 1860. The plan was for an invasion of papal territory by a Piedmontese army which would reach the city of Rome before Garibaldi could. The plot failed because the French would not agree.

Garibaldi had already reached Palermo and been greeted with joyous shouts of 'Rome or Death'. Victor Emmanuel, sensing danger, immediately withdrew his support. No one tried to stop Garibaldi crossing the Straits, for the message sent to the naval commander at Messina was so vague that he ignored it and allowed Garibaldi and his men to cross to Calabria. There, in bad weather, they were shot at by local troops and forced to retreat into the mountains. All except 500 of the men deserted. Those who remained were defeated at Aspromonte in a short battle with government troops at the end of August. Garibaldi, much to his annoyance, was shot in the leg and captured (see the illustration on page 95). He was imprisoned for a time and then returned to Caprera.

Key question
Why did Garibaldi fail to take Rome in 1862?

Garibaldi was defeated at Aspromonte: August 1862

Key date

'Garibaldi Wounded at Aspromonte'. In this painting an Italian general receives the surrender of the wounded Garibaldi. Such was his fame that the bandages around his calf were later venerated by some as sacred relics.

The whole adventure had turned into a disaster for Garibaldi personally and militarily. He was not used to being wounded or to being defeated. The government too was embarrassed that the old hero, one of those responsible for the unification of Italy, had been defeated and imprisoned by the government of the kingdom he had done so much to create.

The second attempt

Key question
Why did Garibaldi fail a second time?

All was not quite over for Garibaldi. In 1864 the Italian government agreed to protect Rome from attack and to remove the Italian capital from Turin in Piedmont to Florence in Tuscany, an indication that the ruling politicians no longer wanted Rome as the capital. In return the French agreed to withdraw their troops from Rome. This arrangement was not popular in Italy, however, as most Italians still wanted 'the Eternal City' as their capital. Riots in Turin left two dozen dead.

Nevertheless the deal was implemented. In April 1865 Florence was proclaimed capital of Italy, and in December 1866 the last French troops duly left Rome. Garibaldi now decided on action. He escaped from house arrest on Caprera and, disguised as a fisherman, sailed in a dinghy across to the mainland where he retook command of his men. Their aim was 'to capture Rome and abolish the Pope'. He hoped that local anti-papal uprisings would take place in Rome. These did not happen, but he and his men marched towards Rome anyway. France sent an army equipped with the new, and very effective, **breech-loading rifles** back to Rome, and when Garibaldi attacked at Mentana on 3 November he was easily defeated. His second attempt to take Rome had ended in complete failure, and as a result the French were back in Rome. This marked the end of Garibaldi's part in Italian history, though not the end of his active life.

Garibaldi defeated at Mentana: 3 November 1867 — Key date

French service

In 1870, after the defeat of Napoleon III by the Prussian army and the end of the Second French Empire, Garibaldi offered his services to the new French Republic. The French government hesitated to accept. After all, Garibaldi was now 63 years old, crippled with arthritis and still troubled by the wound received at Aspromonte. He did not seem the ideal choice for a military leader on active service; but, under pressure from public opinion, the French government appointed him General of the Vosges army, a hotchpotch of sharpshooters and other irregular troops, who managed under Garibaldi's leadership to defeat the Prussians in three small battles.

Afterwards he was elected to the French National Assembly in recognition of his services, but finding his fellow members unfriendly towards him, he returned to his home on the island of Caprera where he remained until his death in 1882.

Meanwhile, French troops having been withdrawn to meet dangers from Prussia at home, Rome had been attacked and captured in 1870 by Italian troops. Garibaldi was distressed that the government should have taken what he thought was unfair advantage of Napoleon III's misfortunes. He felt it was wrong.

Key question
What motivated Garibaldi to work for France?

Death of Garibaldi aged 75: 1882 — Key date

Breech-loading rifles
Rifles whose bullets are loaded through the chamber (or breech) rather than through the barrel (or muzzle). They could be fired four or five times more quickly than muzzle-loaders, and soldiers could load them lying down. — Key term

Summary diagram: Garibaldi and Rome

1862	Garibaldi's first attempt – defeated by Piedmontese forces
1864	Agreement between France and Piedmont
1865	Florence became Italian capital
1866	French troops left Rome
1867	Garibaldi's second attempt – defeated by French forces

4 | Garibaldi: An Assessment

Garibaldi's contribution to the cause of Italian unity was considerable. His flamboyant personality, his striking appearance, his theatricality, his bravery, his legendary adventures both inside and outside Italy, his success with women – all these made him always the centre of attention. He represented the non-intellectual active approach to Italian unity, a very different approach from that of Mazzini or Cavour.

As a soldier

Key question
What accounts for Garibaldi's success as a guerrilla leader?

Garibaldi was a good, sometimes brilliant, commander, excellent at sizing up the situation, decisive and determined. He and his men were best at hand-to-hand fighting, surprise night attacks and ambushes by day. He could appear authoritarian but relied more on his strong personality rather than strict discipline to keep control over his men. Regular Italian officers who visited his camp on the outskirts of Rome in 1849 were shocked by the informality. One of them wrote:

> Garibaldi and his officers were dressed in scarlet blouses with hats of every possible kind, without distinguishing marks and without any military insignia. They rode on [South] American saddles, and seemed to pride themselves on contempt for all the usual military requirements ... they might be seen hurrying to and fro, now dispersing, then again collecting, active, rapid, untiring ... We were surprised to see officers including the General himself leap down from their horses and attend to the wants of their own steeds ... If they failed to obtain provisions from neighbouring villages, three or four colonels and majors threw themselves on the back of their horses and armed with long lassoes set off in search of sheep or oxen.
>   Garibaldi meanwhile ... would lie stretched out under his tent made from his unrolled saddle. If the enemy were at hand he remained constantly on horseback, giving orders and visiting outposts; often, disguised as a peasant, he risked his own safety in daring reconnaissances ... Garibaldi appeared more like the chief of a tribe of Indians than a General, but at the approach of danger, and in the heat of combat, his presence of mind and courage were admirable.

Garibaldi was what we would today call a guerrilla fighter, and as a leader of a guerrilla force he was unrivalled. He inspired great enthusiasm and devotion in his men, firing them with the same passionate belief in Italian unity that he had himself – at least when there was fighting to be done. During times of inaction, or if things became bad, they showed a regrettable tendency to desert. Garibaldi's relaxed style of leadership and the general lack of discipline probably made this inevitable.

It should be realised that an important factor in Garibaldi's military success was the incompetence and lack of enthusiasm shown by the enemy. In Naples in 1860 the king and his troops were so frightened by what Garibaldi had achieved in Sicily that they put up little resistance. In Sicily he had been helped by the general confusion on the island following the peasants' revolt and by local hatred of the remaining Neapolitan troops, who had an unenviable reputation for cruelty.

Nevertheless his conquest of the south was a remarkable achievement and a major element in the successful unification of Italy. He and his men accomplished it almost unaided in a very short time against all odds and expectations.

As a politician

Key question
What were Garibaldi's weaknesses as a politician?

Whether it was wise to unite north and south in this sudden and violent way is another matter. There was support in the south for an end to the rule by an oppressive and absolute monarch (the King of Naples), but this did not mean that there was a demand for union with Piedmont. Garibaldi and his men nearly all came from the north and had little understanding of the problems of the hot, dry south.

Much more could have been done for the peasants, particularly in Sicily. Opportunities to win popular support were missed everywhere. Perhaps if Garibaldi had not conquered southern Italy in his whirlwind campaign, the unsuitable Piedmontese legal and other systems would not have been introduced into southern Italy, certainly not so quickly.

Garibaldi was driven by his devotion to the idea of Italian unity. Everything he did was directed at achieving it. It became an obsession and as a result he could appear to lack principles. From being a republican he had suddenly became a royalist in the service first of Charles Albert and then of Victor Emmanuel; from a supporter of popular revolution he became a supporter of the establishment. In each case he was acting in what he considered to be the best interests of Italian unity. He could have ruled an independent southern Italy himself, but national unity was more important to him than personal power.

He did of course have his limitations. He was not very well educated and not much of a thinker. His greatest weakness was probably his impatience for immediate action. He acted first and thought afterwards, if at all, for his actions were dominated by his heart not his head. His understanding of politics was limited. He was not interested and was often unaware of the effect his actions might have on international relations, as in his plans to march on Rome in 1860, 1862 and 1867. Even if he had been aware of diplomatic repercussions, however, it is doubtful whether he would have been at all concerned.

That chance meeting with Mazzini in 1831 had given him his ideals and his purpose in life. Although he fell out with Mazzini, he never forgot 'Young Italy' or Mazzini's words: 'Without unity there is no true nation, without unity there is no real strength, and Italy, surrounded as she is by powerful, united and jealous nations, has need of strength above all things'. In Garibaldi she found much strength.

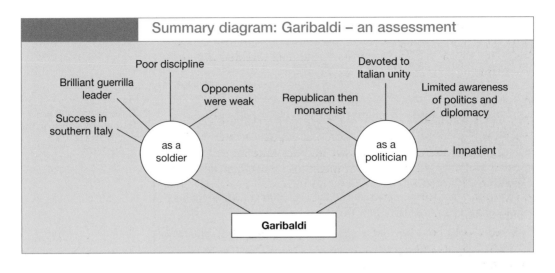

Summary diagram: Garibaldi – an assessment

Study Guide: AS Questions

In the style of AQA

(a) Explain why Garibaldi was forced into exile in 1849.

(12 marks)

(b) 'Garibaldi's actions were crucial to the success of Italian unification.' Explain why you agree or disagree with this view.

(24 marks)

Exam tips

The cross-references are intended to take you straight to the material that will help you to answer the questions.

(a) You should try to provide a variety of factors to explain why Garibaldi was forced into exile. There are a number of obvious reasons:

- because of the failure of the Roman Republic (pages 85–6)
- because Napoleon came to the rescue of the Pope
- because he was caught while trying to lead a march to the coast.

However, there are also more general factors that could be included:

- because Garibaldi was a freedom-fighter, a follower of Mazzini and a supporter of a free, independent and united Italy
- because of his personal charisma and the fear that he could stir up rebellion.

Try to show how these factors link together and to convey your personal judgement as to the extent of the threat Garibaldi posed in 1849 and to whom.

(b) This question is asking you to evaluate Garibaldi's contribution to Italian unification. You should try to think of some details that would agree with the statement and some which would not. You will then need to balance these in your answer, but you should convey a judgement and show which side you find the more convincing. In agreement with the statement you might include:

- Without Garibaldi, unification would only have been in the north (you will need to refer to Cavour's attitude to explain this).
- Garibaldi was the man who was prepared to take a gamble – and he succeeded. He incorporated Sicily and Naples.
- Garibaldi was not afraid to march from the south towards the Papal States.
- He was a popular figure who won people over to the cause of unification.
- He was both a soldier and politician devoted to one cause.
- He was prepared to 'handover' the south and bring about the unification of October 1860 (page 92).

In disagreement with the statement you might include:

- Garibaldi never managed to incorporate Rome – and unification might have 'gone wrong' if he had.
- Venetia remained outside his unification.
- Garibaldi could never have succeeded without Cavour (the Kingdom of North Italy, March 1860).
- Garibaldi was merely a colourful figure – the real groundwork of unification was done by others.

In the style of Edexcel

How far do you agree that Napoleon III was primarily responsible for the success of Piedmontese efforts to drive Austrian influence from Italy in the years 1859–66?   (30 marks)

Exam tips

The cross-references are intended to take you straight to the material that will help you to answer the question.

This question requires you to evaluate the significance of Napoleon III's decisions and actions – these could be what he decided not to do as well as what he did do. The question is not directed generally at why Italy was unified, but specifically at why the Austrians were driven out. The bullet points below give you a number of factors to consider. How will you organise them? Remember to devote about one-third of your answer to the part played by Napoleon III.

- Part of Piedmont's success in freeing Italy from Austrian influence was the war of 1859, in which Piedmont had French help to defeat Austria. This is an immensely important factor, as it was the lack of outside help that had led to Austrian victories over Piedmont in the past. Now, with victories in the field of battle, Austria accepted the expansion of Piedmont and was itself able only to hang on to Venetia in northern Italy. Be sure to concentrate on the essential points and avoid narrative; if you do not you are liable to get bogged down on this single, though vital, factor (see pages 62–3).
- The war of 1859 does not wholly explain Piedmont's success. For a fuller explanation we have to examine the growth of Piedmont, especially its new-found economic power and diplomatic status, after the 1848 revolutions. It became the foremost Italian state, and the most likely to bring about unification (see page 56). We must also be aware of the decline of Austrian power (see page 63).
- Furthermore, we have to examine how the truce of Villafranca, which Cavour so disliked, helped Piedmontese expansion (see page 63).
- Finally, we must look at the diplomatic events of 1866 to see how Venetia, the one and only Austrian stronghold in Italy, became part of the Kingdom of Italy (see pages 114 and 125).

Piedmont's success was clearly due to a combination of factors. Try drawing up a plan that allows you to draw arrows linking factors together and then emphasise their interaction in your answer. Ideally you should reach your conclusion before you begin to actually write your answer. That will give you a greater sense of purpose as you write and should help you to avoid narrative passages. So how significant was Napoleon III?

In the style of OCR

Study the four sources below on the impact of Garibaldi's expedition of 1860, and then answer **both** sub-questions. It is recommended that you spend two-thirds of your time in answering part **(b)**.

(a) Study Sources A and B.
Compare these sources as evidence for the political situation after Garibaldi's conquest of Sicily.   (30 marks)

(b) Study all the sources.
Use your own knowledge to assess how far the sources support the interpretation that Garibaldi's expedition revealed division rather than unity between Italians.   (70 marks)

Source A

From: Cavour's letter to King Victor Emmanuel's Ambassador in Paris, 1 August 1860. Cavour considers what might happen now that Garibaldi has conquered Sicily in May 1860.

If Garibaldi captures Naples, just as he has taken Sicily, he will become master of the situation. King Victor Emmanuel would lose all his prestige in the eyes of Italians, who would see him as little more than the friend of Garibaldi. He would remain a dictator and refuse to join southern Italy to Piedmont. His prestige would then be irresistible. He would be stronger than we are. We would be forced to agree with his plans and help him fight Austria again. Therefore, the king must not receive the crown of Italy from Garibaldi's hands.

Source B

From: Count Trecchi, An Anthology of Letters, 5 August 1860. Victor Emmanuel sends a message to Garibaldi.

When Garibaldi reaches Naples, he must do whatever circumstances suggest: he could occupy the central Papal States. Once in Naples he should proclaim union with the rest of Italy, just as he has done in Sicily. He must prevent disorder, for that would harm our cause. He should keep the Bourbon army in being and ready, for Austria might declare war on us shortly. He should let the King of Naples escape; or, if the King should be captured by the people, Garibaldi should protect him and let him escape.

Source C

From: an account of the session of the Chamber of Deputies in the Parliament of Italy, 18 April 1861. Garibaldi clashes with Cavour in parliament.

Garibaldi: Italy is not divided, she is whole; I and my friends will always champion Italy's cause. (Cheers.) I must remind you of the glorious deeds of the Southern Army. My hopes for unity were ruined by the government when they sent forces against us. (*Protests from the Ministers' bench and violent exchanges within the Chamber.*)

Cavour: It is unpardonable to insult us in this way. Our intentions were always honourable. (*Applause from the Deputies' benches and the galleries.*) Mr Chairman! See to it that the government of the nation is respected! Call people to order! (*Interruptions.*)

Source D

From: A. Stiles, The Unification of Italy, *published in 1986. A modern historian assesses the impact of Garibaldi's expedition.*

There was support in the south for liberation from an oppressive monarchy but not necessarily a wish for unity with the north. Most of Garibaldi's men came from the north and had little sympathy for the impoverished and backward south. If Garibaldi had been less anxious to move north so quickly, more might have been done for the peasants instead of, as in Sicily, abandoning them to the landlords. An opportunity was missed to win popular support through agrarian reform. If the relationship between Garibaldi and Cavour had been different the outcome might have been better.

Exam tips

The cross-references are designed to take you straight to the
material that will help you to answer the questions.

Read the 'General Introduction' section at the start of the study
guide in Chapter 2, page 46.

(a) As stated in the exam tips for Chapter 3, don't compare the
sources one at a time, but compare them simultaneously, theme
by theme or point by point as evidence for the political situation
at that time, e.g. Source A regards Garibaldi as a potential threat
to the position of Victor Emmanuel whereas in Source B the king
is giving him instructions. Further, the king in Source B appears
to be calm and confident about what will happen next whereas
Cavour in Source A is very alarmed.

   The sources show two very different ways in which Italy might
be unified: Source B under Piedmontese leadership and
·direction, whereas Cavour in Source A is afraid that Garibaldi will
overshadow Piedmont and will be able to direct the unification
process himself. These two sources do not say what will happen
– both refer to the future, although Victor Emmanuel is trying to
make it happen by giving Garibaldi orders in Source B. In reality,
was he afraid, just like Cavour in Source A? If so, was his
message (Source B) an attempt to take command of the
situation? Certainly Source A does not share the optimism of
Source B about Garibaldi's political intentions. But might that
reflect a difference more apparent than real? In a private letter,
Cavour could express his thoughts clearly and fully whereas
what the king said would become public, and be seen by or at
least reported to Garibaldi himself. Victor Emmanuel had to be
careful.

(b) This question is the more important part. Hence you must read
the other two extracts and gather from them the information that
relates to the key issue: whether Garibaldi's expedition reveals
unity or division among Italians. Source C obviously shows
disagreement. Not only do Cavour and Garibaldi clash, but – as
we can see from the reactions of the Deputies and the citizens
in the galleries, with cheers from one side alternating with
applause from the other – the wider political community does as
well. Source D adds to the 'division' side. It points out key
differences between north and south. Sicily and Naples did
indeed declare for union, but their real aim had been to throw off
oppressive Bourbon rule not to take part in '*Italia una*' (see
pages 71 and 124).

   You must bring in Sources C and D, but don't neglect A and
B. Garibaldi's expedition certainly reveals the differences
between the adventurer and the politician, and to some degree
between the king and his prime minister (see pages 69 and 145).

Furthermore, you must use your own knowledge. Other points you must address include:

- The divisions not just between north and south but, within southern Italy, between the inhabitants of Sicily and Naples (see page 88).
- The fact that Garibaldi and his 'Thousand' were fighting other Italians (see page 89).
- The vexed issue of the Papal States and of Rome. Garibaldi undoubtedly wanted to press on northwards from Naples and to unite the whole of Italy. Cavour was determined to stop him (see pages 69–71); so was the Pope, who of course was also an Italian.

Make sure that, at the end of your answer, you come to some sort of conclusion. Clearly Garibaldi's expedition served the cause of Italian unification; of that there can be no doubt. But did it reveal division rather than unity? Most of us would answer yes and no; yes in some respects, no in others. (Remember that Garibaldi had his arguments with Cavour but that, even so, he thought of himself as a loyal Italian and he did hand over Sicily and Naples to Victor Emmanuel.) First you have to decide your view, and then you have to find a form of words that expresses your opinion as clearly as possible.

5 Napoleon III and Italy

POINTS TO CONSIDER

It has already been established that France played a major role in the unification of Italy. This chapter examines the precise part played by France, and more especially by the Emperor Napoleon III, through the following sections:

- Louis Napoleon: romantic adventurer
- Louis Napoleon and the Roman Republic
- 'Doing something for Italy'
- Napoleon and the unification of Italy

There are two particularly important issues to grapple with. The first is why Napoleon III of France was interested in what was happening in Italy. Was this notorious conspirator and wheeler-dealer more concerned with the interests of his own country rather than those of Italy? The second concerns the effects his policies had. Was his input crucial to eventual Italian unification? Might unification have been achieved without French involvement?

Key dates

1849	July	Rome fell to French forces
1852	December	Louis Napoleon became Emperor Napoleon III
1858	January 14	Orsini tried but failed to assassinate Napoleon III
1858	July 21	Meeting at Plombières between Napoleon III and Cavour
1859		France and Piedmont went to war with Austria, winning the battles of Magenta and Solferino
1866	July 3	Battle of Königgrätz
	August	Peace of Prague
1870	July	Start of the Franco-Prussian War
	September 20	Italian troops entered Rome

1 | Louis Napoleon: Romantic Adventurer

Key question
What in Louis
Napoleon's
background made
him a romantic
adventurer?

Key term

Regent
A person appointed
to administer a
state whose
monarch is unable
to do so.

The family of Napoleon Bonaparte (the Emperor Napoleon I) was exiled from France by the Vienna Settlement of 1815 (see page 8). Some of its members were in Italy during the winter of the revolutionary year 1830–1 (see page 23). Among them was the 22-year-old Louis Napoleon Bonaparte, Napoleon I's nephew, who became involved in a wild and foolish scheme, involving the capture of the Pope's castle of Saint Angelo, to proclaim his cousin, the son of Napoleon I, as King of Italy. Since this cousin was in fact a prisoner of the Austrians, Louis Napoleon would have ruled as **regent** on his behalf. Yet the secret was not well kept and the authorities had little difficulty in discovering the plot and arresting those involved.

Louis Napoleon was expelled from Rome and went to join the rest of his family in Florence. Here he almost immediately became entangled in another conspiracy involving Modena and the Papal States. Clearly the young Louis Napoleon did not intend to lead a 'normal' life. He was full of romantic, impracticable dreams and schemes, but with perhaps genuine and certainly vague liberal ideas. Conspiracy, adventure and the search for power and prestige seemed to be part of his heritage.

The conspiracies of 1830–1 mark the beginning of Louis Napoleon's love affair with Italian nationalism. Although his actions were often unpredictable, and although there was an element of self-interest in many of the things he did, it was to be with his aid, in the end, that Italian independence and unity were achieved in 1859–60 (see pages 62–7).

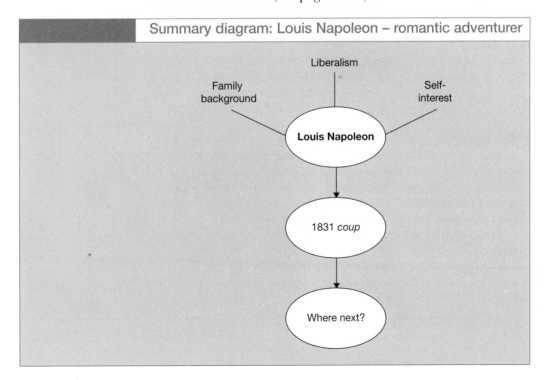

Summary diagram: Louis Napoleon – romantic adventurer

Profile: Louis Napoleon Bonaparte, Napoleon III 1808–73

1808		– Born in Paris, the third son Louis Bonaparte, the brother of Napoleon I. Brought up in exile in Switzerland
1831		– Expelled from Rome after attempted *coup*
1832		– Became head of the Napoleonic **dynasty**
1836 and 1840		– Involved in two failed *coups* in Paris
1848	December	– Elected President of the French Republic
1849	March–July	– His forces destroyed the Roman Republic
1852	December	– Became Emperor of France after a successful *coup*. At home, he encouraged economic expansion; abroad, he sought glory and prestige
1854–6		– Involved in Crimean War. He was on the winning side against Russia
1859		– Defeated Austria and furthered the cause of Italian independence
1860		– Gained Nice and Savoy for France
1862–5		– Intervention in Mexico ended in disaster
1870–1		– Franco-Prussian War
1871		– Went into exile in England, where he lived until his death
1873		– Died

Dynasty
A succession of powerful rulers from the same family.

Key term

Controversy has always surrounded the career of Louis Napoleon, especially the issue of his motives, including why he supported the cause of Italian unification. The fact that he was a member of the Bonaparte family is crucial here. 'When a man of my name is in power', he insisted, 'he must do great things'. At least he had to *try* to do great things. Also hotly debated is the level of ability he possessed. The leader of Prussia, and then Germany, Otto von Bismarck, was certainly not impressed with him. After one meeting he wrote the following about Napoleon III: 'Far afar, something; near at hand, nothing: a great, unfathomed incapacity'.

Key question
Why did Napoleon destroy Mazzini's regime in Rome?

Key date

Rome fell to French forces: July 1849

Key terms

Expeditionary force
A small army dispatched for a particular mission.

Clericalist
Supporting the Catholic Church, its clergy and its policies.

2 | Louis Napoleon and the Roman Republic

In the 1830s Louis Napoleon's wish to help the Italians seemed sincere, but in March 1849, when the Roman Republic was proclaimed with Mazzini at its head and Garibaldi as its military leader (see page 37), he reacted very differently, as a counter-revolutionary rather than a supporter of nationalism. He was now no longer a hopeful rebel, having been elected President of the French Republic a few months earlier.

Pius IX fled Rome during the revolutions of 1848 and took refuge in Naples. He appealed to the Catholic monarchs of Europe, but no help came. Yet Louis Napoleon was prepared to act. He knew that the Austrians, who were already occupying Tuscany and the northern part of the Papal States, would soon be threatening Rome itself. There was no time to lose: he could benefit from the situation by restoring the Pope and winning the approval of the Church which would follow from this.

The French Assembly agreed to Napoleon's plan of providing an **expeditionary force** to be sent to Rome, and 10,000 troops set sail in April 1849. Their commander was well received when they landed in the Papal States near Rome and confidently expected a similar welcome from the citizens of Rome itself. He was not prepared for the strong resistance organised by Mazzini and Garibaldi. Louis Napoleon then agreed to an armistice, but only to buy time. A Bonaparte could not begin his Presidency of France with a military defeat or a meek compromise. Hence he reinforced his army, and soon over 20,000 French soldiers attacked. Rome fell in July.

The consequences

In a sense, Napoleon had succeeded. Papal rule had been restored, as he intended, the Austrians had been kept at bay, and at home he received support from **clericalist** forces. Yet the heir of the revolutionary Napoleon Bonaparte had made himself the champion of the most illiberal regime in Europe, that of Pope Pius IX, and Rome was quickly restored to the reactionary government of the papal governing body, the Curia.

The government of Rome was again as it had been: backward and oppressive. There were loud complaints in the French assembly at this betrayal of republican principles. What is more, Napoleon himself realised he had made a grave error. His first action in foreign policy had been to restore the temporal power of the papacy, which he himself, in 1830, had tried to remove. Such an action was unworthy of a Bonaparte. He would have to achieve more worthy successes in the future.

Summary diagram: Louis Napoleon and the Roman Republic

March 1849 – setting up of the Roman Republic

July 1849 – French troops ended the Republic

Louis Napoleon's motives: • anti-Austrian move?
• need for a success?
• need to win clericalist support at home?

3 | 'Doing Something for Italy'

In December 1852 Napoleon assumed the title of Emperor Napoleon III. He declared that France wanted peace, but quickly found himself fighting against Russia in defence of Turkey in the Crimean War, which broke out in 1854. Among France's allies was Piedmont, and when the war ended, in 1856, Cavour too had a seat at the peace conference in Paris. This brought the two men into close contact, with important long-term consequences for them both. After the conference ended, they kept in touch through mutual friends and through Napoleon's nephew, a doctor who treated them both, Cavour's private secretary, and the young and beautiful **Countess Castiglione**.

Napoleon's intentions

On a number of occasions in the 1850s Napoleon spoke to Cavour about 'doing something for Italy' but did not explain what that something was. It is difficult to know what, if anything, he had in mind. Certainly, if he had any plans, they were at this stage vague and capable of being changed at any moment. And, of course, they were secret, making it extremely difficult to unravel them.

It is generally assumed that he saw his main enemy as being Austria, since Austria had taken the lead at the Congress of Vienna in undoing the work of Napoleon I (see page 9) and was the leading conservative power in Europe and the natural enemy of France. As part of his anti-Austrian policy, Napoleon III wished at least to weaken Austria's hold on northern Italy.

It may have been that, as a romantic but sincere supporter of Italian independence, Napoleon wished to be helpful to the cause. After all, in 1830 he had been a *Carbonaro* (see page 20), or something of the kind. He may also have been influenced by family tradition: Napoleon I had taken over Italy at the beginning of the nineteenth century. Hence the nephew would be continuing the Napoleonic legend. Although he had none of the qualities, the determination and the gifts of leadership that Napoleon I had possessed, he saw himself as a leader of 'the

Key question
What was the probable mix of motives that influenced Napoleon's actions in Italy?

Key date

Louis Napoleon became Emperor Napoleon III: December 1852

Key figure

Countess Virginia di Castiglione 1837–99
A 19-year-old whom Cavour sent to Paris to seduce the Emperor. Napoleon slept with her, considering her 'very pretty but with no charm'.

peoples of Europe' in their search for freedom and national identity. As for the episode of the Roman Republic in 1849, that was best forgotten.

Napoleon's self-interest

Yet it is very easy to see an element of self-interest in Napoleon's views. Admittedly he wished to drive the Austrians out of Italy and help to create an enlarged Piedmont. But this new Piedmont, though large enough to be a useful ally for France, should not become so large as to act independently of France, to oppose French wishes or to be a threat to France itself. It must certainly not be allowed to become strong enough to interfere with French ambitions to acquire Nice and Savoy. The return of these areas, once part of Napoleon I's territory, would be a tangible sign of

Napoleon III on horseback.

his success. According to his critics, Napoleon III simply wished to replace Austrian influence in Italy with French, and thus he was more a French imperialist than a true supporter of Italian nationalism – a criticism that had also been levelled against his uncle.

Napoleon's solution?

Also, we have to ask what Napoleon III meant when he talked about 'Italy'. Some historians believe that before 1861 'Italy' to him meant northern Italy, the old Napoleonic Kingdom of Italy, made up of states such as Piedmont, already substantially French in character as a consequence of the occupying forces at the beginning of the century, and where French was still the language of the educated minority. At this stage it is doubtful whether Napoleon would have wanted the whole Italian peninsula united into a single kingdom. After all, such a united country might become a threat to France itself.

What of central Italy? This could become part of the new Piedmont or a separate French-controlled state, perhaps governed by one of Napoleon's many cousins. Other cousins could rule Naples and Sicily. The Pope would be persuaded to agree to all these arrangements by being made President of an Italian Federation of States (see page 60).

This scenario seemed to Napoleon a splendid idea which would appeal to almost everyone:

- to Italian nationalists, because the Austrians had been driven out
- to moderate nationalists, as the old absolute governments would disappear
- to Victor Emmanuel and Cavour, as Piedmont would be expanded
- to the clergy, as the political power of the Pope would grow
- to French nationalists, by the acquisition of new territory and the replacement of Austrian influence in Italy by that of France
- to the Bonaparte family, by an extension of their power and prestige.

This arrangement might well have been Napoleon's ideal solution to the Italian question. But would the French Emperor be motivated enough to attempt to make it a reality?

The Orsini affair

Napoleon moved into action in January 1858, when an attempt was made on his life. A group of four Italians, led by **Count Felice Orsini**, was responsible. Orsini had been a refugee in London, where he had had three large bombs specially made for him. The men took the bombs from London to Paris via Brussels, by train, completely outwitting the French police who had been tipped off that they would be arriving by road. The bombs were thrown at Napoleon and the Empress Eugénie as their coach arrived at the opera. Eight people died and about 150 were injured, but the Emperor and his wife were unharmed.

Key figure

Count Felice Orsini 1819–58 An Italian patriot and follower of Mazzini, had been elected a member of the Roman assembly in 1848 and, under Garibaldi, had taken part in the defence of the city against the French. He was executed after the assassination attempt.

Key question
Why did the assassination plot on his life lead Napoleon to take up the cause of Italian nationalism?

Key date
Orsini tried but failed to assassinate Napoleon III: 14 January 1858

Orsini seems to have believed that if he killed Napoleon a new republican government in France would come to the assistance of Italy. At his trial, a letter, said to have been written by Orsini in his prison cell, was read out. In it Orsini appealed to Napoleon to help Italy to achieve independence and by doing so to receive the blessings of 25 million Italian citizens. There is some evidence that Napoleon himself encouraged Orsini to write this letter and may even have dictated its contents. He certainly arranged for it to be published. It is still not known whether the letter was a genuine plea from an Italian patriot or whether it was organised by Napoleon to provide him with an excuse to intervene in Italy.

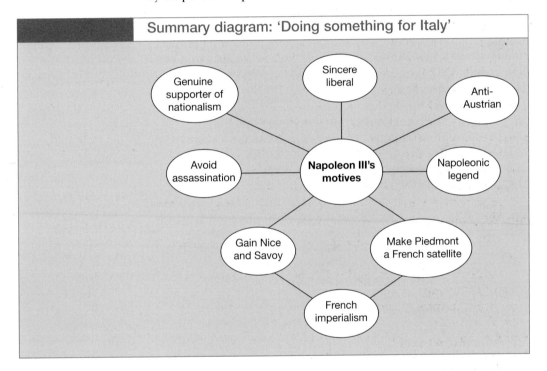

Summary diagram: 'Doing something for Italy'

4 | Napoleon and the Unification of Italy

The war against Austria 1859

Key question
How crucial was French support to the growth and eventual unification of Italy?

Napoleon wasted no time. Perhaps he was genuinely impressed by Orsini's letter. Perhaps he feared that, unless he took action, further assassination attempts might be made. Perhaps he just saw the opportunity to gain prestige. In any event, he would now do something for Italy, and for France.

He began by meeting Cavour at Plombières on 21 July 1858, where they hatched the plot to try to lure Austria into war (see pages 59–61). Napoleon agreed that providing a suitable excuse for war could be devised, he would support Piedmont in an attempt to drive the Austrians out of northern Italy. The result was the war of 1859 and an expanded Piedmont. Events did not work out as smoothly as Napoleon had hoped, however. In particular, the battles – at Solferino and Magenta – proved far more destructive than anticipated, while Piedmont became more

Key dates

Meeting at Plombières between Napoleon III and Cavour: 21 July 1858

France and Piedmont went to war with Austria, winning battles of Magenta and Solferino: 1859

powerful than he had expected. But at least France received Nice and Savoy and Austrian power in Italy was greatly weakened (see pages 62–5 for details of the 'Second War of Independence').

Garibaldi and Rome

After Garibaldi's successful conquest of Sicily in July 1860 (see page 89), the European powers woke up to the fact that he clearly intended to attack the Neapolitan mainland. Should he be allowed to do so? This was the question being asked in diplomatic circles everywhere.

Key question
What was Napoleon's attitude to Garibaldi's successes in southern Italy?

In a flurry of activity only Britain among the Great Powers had any sympathy with Garibaldi's aims. Napoleon found himself in difficulties. He did not want to offend Britain by trying to stop Garibaldi, but he did not want to see Garibaldi take over Naples and threaten Rome and the Pope. He suggested to Britain a **naval blockade** of the Straits of Messina to make it impossible for Garibaldi to leave Sicily for the mainland. But Britain refused and Garibaldi crossed the Straits successfully in the middle of August, meeting only token resistance from the Neapolitan navy.

When Cavour's army entered the Papal States on 11 September to prevent Garibaldi and his army from reaching Rome, Napoleon had to disapprove in public of what was no less than the unprovoked invasion of a neighbouring state. However, he had made a secret agreement with Cavour that France would not interfere as long as Garibaldi did not reach Rome. French diplomatic relations with Piedmont were broken off, but this seems to have been a gesture by Napoleon and not meant to be taken seriously. He did nothing to prevent the degree of Italian unification that was complete by 1860: the whole of the peninsula, apart from Venetia and Rome, became part of Victor Emmanuel II's kingdom of Italy.

Key terms

Naval blockade
The use of ships to prevent people or goods entering or leaving ports.

Second front
An alternative scene of battle, generally diverting the enemy's attention from the major focus of a war

Venetia and Rome
Venetia

In 1866 the question of Venetia came to a head. First, in April, Italy signed an alliance with Prussia, whose prime minister, Otto von Bismarck, was engaged in a struggle with Austria for control of Germany. Italy agreed that if Prussia went to war with Austria within the next few months, Italy would follow Prussia and declare war on Austria.

Key question
What role did Napoleon III play in adding Venetia and Rome to the new Italian state?

Secondly, Napoleon III signed a secret treaty with Bismarck in June. Not only would France remain neutral in an Austro-Prussian war, but at the end of the conflict France would receive Venetia if Austria were defeated. This would then be given by Napoleon to Italy as a reward for providing a **second front** in the Austro-Prussian war. Once again Napoleon III would be the sponsor of Italian nationalism, winning the gratitude of an Italian government which, he hoped, would be compliant to French wishes. Furthermore, he would gain international prestige by his generosity in favour of a liberal cause.

Knowing now that Italy would receive Venetia if Prussia won, Napoleon – with great diplomatic skill and also total lack of principle, the two often going together – needed to make sure that the same thing would happen if Austria won. He therefore signed a secret treaty with Austria in which it was agreed that if Austria defeated Prussia, Venetia would be ceded to France and passed on by Napoleon to Italy. In return France would remain neutral during the war.

The war of 1866

Key dates

Battle of Königgrätz: 3 July 1866

Peace of Prague: August 1866

Start of the Franco-Prussian War: July 1870

The war, known in Germany as the Seven Weeks' War and in Italy as the Third War of Independence, began on 24 June 1866. Italian confidence was high, but their army was defeated by a smaller Austrian force at the (second) battle of Custoza 10 days later, largely owing to poor Italian generalship. But this was really no more than a side-show.

The decisive battle was fought on 3 July by Austria and Prussia at Königgrätz, also known as Sadowa. It was a horrific encounter. According to an eyewitness account, bombs crashed around the Prussian soldiers 'through walls of clay as if they were cardboard … Chunks of wood and big tree splinters flew around our heads.' Austrian soldiers too suffered when 4000 men set out to attack the Prussian guns, a venture from which only 1800 badly wounded men returned. Many Austrian soldiers tried to reach the safety of the town of Königgrätz, only to be drowned in water released from the waterworks which protected the town. As before, there was inadequate provision for looking after the wounded, who were left lying for up to three days on the 45 square miles of the battlefield. The Prussians lost almost 2000 men, the Austrians nearer 6000.

The war came to an end with the Peace of Prague in August 1866. By it, Austria immediately gave up Venetia to Napoleon, who in turn surrendered it, as agreed, to Italy.

Welcome as the return of Venetia was, there was a feeling of humiliation in Italy about the way in which it had been done, not by Italians, but only as the result of action by the Great Powers of Austria, Prussia and France. At least Italians could console themselves with the thought that, once Rome was also recovered, Italian unification would be complete.

Rome

Key question
By what process was Rome added to Italy?

The outstanding problem now was how to get rid of the French garrison in Rome. Only then would the work of driving out the foreigners be complete. How could it be done? Again success stemmed not from Italy's own strength but from the international situation.

In 1870 the Franco-Prussian War broke out. Conflict had been brewing between the two rival powers for some time, and in July Bismarck skilfully manoeuvred Napoleon III into declaring war on Prussia, a conflict that the Prussian leader used to whip up nationalist feeling and to unify Germany.

In an unexpected piece of good fortune for Italy, very soon after the war began Napoleon needed reinforcements to bring his army up to strength and so withdrew his troops from Rome. The Italian government made no immediate move to take over the city, but after 1 September 1870 – when Napoleon was heavily defeated at the battle of Sedan and was taken prisoner by the Prussians – they felt it safe to take action.

Victor Emmanuel, whose daughter was married to Napoleon's cousin, felt that he ought to send an army to rescue Napoleon, but his government thought otherwise. Italy had been neutral in the war and must remain so. This did not mean, though, that they could not take advantage of Napoleon's misfortunes to settle the question of Rome once and for all.

On 8 September Victor Emmanuel sent a letter to the Pope suggesting an agreement. The Pope would have to give up his temporal power, which since 1849 had depended on the support of the French troops in Rome, and allow Rome to become at last the capital of a united Italy. In return he would be allowed to keep his spiritual power as head of the Church which would be safeguarded and guaranteed by the Italian state.

Three days later the Pope rejected this arrangement. As a result, the government decided to act. An army of 6000 troops was sent to occupy Rome. Papal troops fought back briefly but the city was shelled by government artillery and a breach made in the walls. On 20 September 1870 Victor Emmanuel's army entered Rome. In October Roman citizens voted overwhelmingly (by 133,681 to 1507) for union with the rest of Italy, and Rome became the capital city of a politically and geographically united Italy.

The new Kingdom of Italy seemed to be complete. That it was still severely flawed socially, economically and politically was not acknowledged, least of all by 'King Victor Emmanuel II of Italy' (not, it should be noted, King Victor Emmanuel I, although he was the first king of a united Italy). At the first session of the first parliament to be held in the new capital, disregarding the still unsolved problem of what to do about the Pope, the king declared: 'The work to which we consecrated our lives is accomplished'.

Key date

Italian troops entered Rome: 20 September 1870

Summary diagram: Napoleon and the unification of Italy

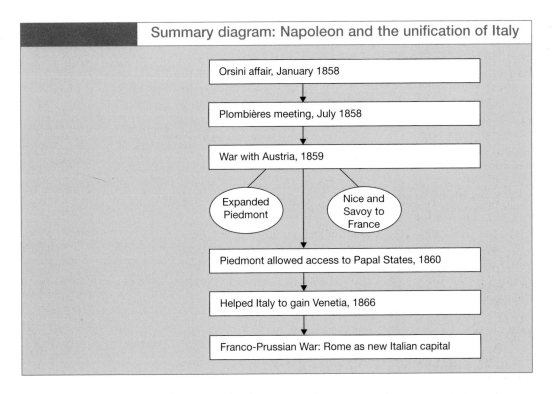

Study Guide: AS Questions

In the style of AQA

(a) Explain why Napoleon III wanted to 'do something for Italy' in the 1850s. (12 marks)

(b) 'Napoleon III was the true champion of Italian unification between 1859 and 1870.' Explain why you agree or disagree with this view. (24 marks)

Exam tips

The cross-references are intended to take you straight to the material that will help you to answer the questions.

(a) Start by re-reading pages 110–12 and making a list of factors which could explain Napoleon's interest in the Italian question:

- his enmity towards Austria
- his sincere support for Italian unification
- his desire to have Piedmont as an ally
- his quest for prestige
- his desire for more territory
- his wish to curry favour with the Pope
- the Orsini affair.

You will probably want to argue that some of these reasons are more important than others and there may be some you wish to dismiss. Decide your priorities before you begin writing and don't forget to show the links between the factors. You should also provide an overall conclusion.

(b) This question is asking you to assess Napoleon III's contribution to Italian unification by considering one interpretation of his actions. You will need to think of ways in which Napoleon III was involved in the moves towards unification in these years and decide whether they agree or disagree with the statement. You might include:

- The French war against Austria, undertaken to support Piedmont but concluded before Piedmont had achieved its aims.
- Napoleon III was determined to prevent Garibaldi entering Rome, although he allowed Cavour to enter the Papal States in September 1860 (pages 109–13) and didn't stop unification in 1860.
- In 1866 his actions allowed Venetia to be incorporated into the united Italy, but he had his own agenda (pages 114–15).
- He allowed the incorporation of Rome, but only after he was forced to withdraw troops; hardly a championing of a cause.

You might want to consider how far Napoleon III's actions reflect a championing of the Italian cause and how far they were undertaken with French interests first and foremost (pages 110–11).

In the style of Edexcel

To what extent did France promote the unification of Italy from 1848 to 1870? (30 marks)

Exam tips

The cross-references are intended to take you straight to the material that will help you to answer the question.

France was vital to the process of Italian unification. Within the 1848–70 time-frame, the following episodes are clearly important:

- The ending of the Roman Republic by French troops in 1849 (see pages 37–8).
- The 1858–60 period when Napoleon III and Cavour agreed to work together and fought the war of 1859 against Austria. Napoleon also turned a blind eye when Cavour moved Piedmont's troops through the Papal States in order to head off Garibaldi (see pages 113–14).
- Napoleon's help in securing Venetia for Italy, as a result of the 1866 Austro-Prussian war (see pages 114–15).
- The Franco-Prussian War of 1870–1, which saw French troops leave Rome.

You will need to mention all of the above, but do not forget that the question focuses on the extent to which France actually *promoted* Italian unification. France's actions, as in its withdrawal from Rome in 1870, may have served the cause of Italian unity, but Napoleon III may not have consciously sought this unity. The key years are 1858–60, and here you should not only say what happened but also comment on the French Emperor's motives. Was he trying to promote French interests in Italy, aiming to secure an expanded Piedmont as a French client state (see pages 110–11)?

Finally, as this is a 'to what extent' question, you should weigh up France's promotion of Italian unity alongside the other factors involved, including Italians' promotion of Italian unity. How relatively important was the French connection?

In the style of OCR

Study the four sources and then answer **both** sub-questions. It is recommended that you spend two-thirds of your time in answering part **(b)**.

(a) **Study Sources A and B.**
 Compare these sources as evidence for the role Italians expected France to play in Italy. (30 marks)

(b) **Study all the sources.**
 Use your own knowledge to assess how far the sources support the interpretation that Napoleon III was an obstacle to the unification of Italy. (70 marks)

Source A

From: Felice Orsini in a letter to Napoleon III. The Italian revolutionary nationalist explains the Italian situation to the French Emperor in February 1858.

You have destroyed liberty in my country. However, in the present state of Europe you can decide whether Italy is free or the slave of Austria. I would not ask that French blood should be shed for Italians. Instead, we ask that France should not intervene against us, and should not allow other nations to intervene in the struggle against Austria. The happiness or unhappiness of my country depends on you. I beg you to give Italy again the independence that Frenchmen helped her to lose in 1849. Neither Europe nor Your Majesty can expect peace until Italy is free.

Source B

From: the terms of the agreement made between Piedmont and France following discussions at Plombières, July 1858. The Franco-Piedmontese Treaty, January 1859.

Article 1   If aggression by Austria leads to war between Piedmont and Austria an alliance will come into force between France and Piedmont.

Article 2   The alliance will aim to liberate Italy from Austrian occupation, to satisfy the wishes of the people to create a Kingdom of Upper Italy and bring peace to Europe.

Article 3   Savoy and Nice will be reunited with France.

Article 4   The interests of the Catholic religion and the sovereignty of the Pope shall be maintained.

Article 5   The cost of war will be met by Italy.

Article 6   Neither side will make peace without the agreement of the other.

Source C

From: L. Seaman, From Vienna to Versailles, *published in 1955. A modern historian assesses the contribution of Napoleon III to Italian unification.*

The Villafranca proposals dissatisfied the Piedmontese, yet secured for them more than they could have got if Napoleon had stayed at home. Also, the decisions of Napoleon achieved the annexation of Lombardy and ensured that the Duchies and the Romagna were not returned to their legitimate rulers. The work of Cavour in the north and the centre of Italy up to April 1860 depended completely on Napoleon's initiative in attacking the Habsburgs. Garibaldi's verdict after Villafranca was fair: 'Do not forget the gratitude we owe to Napoleon.'

Source D

*A cartoon comments on the armistice at Villafranca in July 1859.
The figures (from left to right) represent Austria, Italy and France.
From* Punch, *23 July 1859.*

FREE ITALY (?)

Source: adapted from OCR, June 2007

Exam tips

Read the 'General Introduction' section at the start of the study guide
in Chapter 2, page 46.

(a) Remember what the question asked you to do: compare these
two sources '*as evidence for* the role Italians expected the
French to play', so stick to that – comparison of points that do
not provide such evidence may be true but will be irrelevant.

While both agree that France will support the Italians in the
struggle that would be necessary to expel Austria if Italy was to
be free, various differences can be discussed – the objective is
the creation of a Kingdom of Italy (Source A) versus the less
ambitious objective of the creation of a Kingdom of North Italy

(Source B); France should (Source A) or should not (Source B) intervene to bring about Italian independence; Italy will fight alone for independence (Source A) or French troops will help by fighting in Piedmont (Source B).

Consider the significance of the date of each. You should also use provenance and context to help to explain these differences: Orsini in Source A reflects the romantic idealism of revolutionary Italian nationalists like the followers of Mazzini and Young Italy, whereas Source B represents the more practical position of Italian politicians like Cavour, negotiating an international treaty. For Orsini the idealist (Source A), Italy will act alone and France is a potential obstacle that must be persuaded to remain neutral, whereas Cavour (Source B) has learned from the failures of 1848–9 and knows that external assistance will be essential to success in the coming struggle with Austria. Further, Orsini (Source A) is trying to catch Napoleon's interest and persuade the French ruler by appealing to his self-interest whereas the very precise, functional details of Source B are explained by the fact that it follows the agreement already made at Plombières in 1858. Thus the Piedmontese politician and nationalist Cavour (Source B) focuses on a northern Italian state and is willing to leave the Papal States alone and to surrender Nice and Savoy to France. The scales of the ambition shown for the new Italy in Sources A and B are thus very different.

Don't wander off the question by explaining Orsini's background or his fate.

(b) Read the whole question properly. Don't see the words 'own knowledge' and then ignore the sources and wander off into an 'ordinary' essay. The command is very clear: 'Use your own knowledge to assess how far the sources support the interpretation …'.

Group the sources according to what they say, what they agree on and what they disagree on, and then test each aspect against what you know. Sources A and D see Napoleon as an obstacle while Sources B and C illustrate his positive role in unification. Which view makes for a better fit with the facts, and why?

Now look again at that grouping. If you read Sources A and B carefully, both can be used either way in this argument. Sources A, B and C show Napoleon obstructing unification at Villafranca, while Sources A and D show it again over Rome. On the other hand, Sources A, B and C testify to Napoleon's help, especially in 1859. So, you need to offer a more sophisticated answer than 'yes' or 'no'.

So what of your 'own knowledge' can you bring into play to help you decide 'how far'? On Napoleon as an obstacle, perhaps the obvious starting point is to consider what Napoleon agreed to at Villafranca against the treaty that he had made earlier that year after Plombières (Source B). You could link this to the Treaty of Zurich that he then made, depriving Piedmont of the Duchies and two of the quadrilateral fortresses, Mantua and Peschiera, and threatening further Italian unification with a proposed European Congress.

What about the reference to helping Italy to lose its independence in 1849 (Source A)? You could judge the accuracy of that by considering the event it refers to – the army of 20,000 that Napoleon sent to destroy the Roman Republic and restore papal rule. Might the revolutionary nationalist Orsini exaggerate? If he does, the cartoon (Source D) makes exactly the same point about Napoleon: he is more interested in supporting the Catholic Church than in uniting Italy; Article 4, which he insisted upon (Source B), could also be used in support. You could go on to refer to the French garrison in Rome until 1870, and the reinforcements that Napoleon sent in 1867 against Garibaldi's attempt to take the city and add it to the Italian kingdom. Napoleon kept Rome out of Italy throughout the 1860s.

Don't forget the other side of the issue. What of Napoleon's help in bringing about Italian unification? Source C is very strongly in favour of such a view, and we have already noted that Sources A, B and D all have parts that support such an interpretation. Orsini (Source A), the man who had tried to assassinate Napoleon, argues that everything depends on the French emperor while the quotation from Garibaldi in Source C is very powerful evidence from a central nationalist figure that Napoleon had indeed fulfilled that hope. Garibaldi's opinion must be taken seriously. What do you know that explains Garibaldi's assertion? You could refer to the key role played by the provision of 20,000 French troops in 1859 and their critical role in the battles that year while, in contrast, noting that Piedmont's army suffered defeats in 1848, 1849 and 1866. On the battlefield, self-help (*Italia fara da sè*) was not going to win freedom. You could go on to point out Napoleon's key role in supporting the Italian annexation of Venetia in 1865. Garibaldi had in mind the military and diplomatic help that Napoleon gave to Italy in 1859 and in 1865–6. Obstacle or asset? Clearly he was both. You have to decide how the balance tips between the one and the other.

As a final note. In evaluating the cartoon (Source D), stick to the point. Examiners see plenty of irrelevant text (e.g. in this case, comments on moustaches or Napoleon's weight, which have nothing to do with answering the question). What can you say about it? It makes a strong condemnation of Napoleon's behaviour at Villafranca – look at Italy, still chained to Austria; look at the oversize papal crown that dwarfs Italy and will weigh it down. Equally, you should note that the cartoon is from Britain, a country strongly pro-Italian unification and strongly anti-Catholic, so it hardly takes a neutral view. But that is the value of cartoons for historians – they put over a simplified message, in exaggerated form, to make their point, so they are excellent ways for us to test the temperature and know just how strong the views were (prejudices) of one key group or another. Their very bias makes them such useful evidence.

6 The Kingdom of Italy 1861–70

POINTS TO CONSIDER

This chapter considers the condition of the Italian people during the years between the proclamation of the Kingdom of Italy in 1861 and the events that finally completed the process of unification in 1870. It assesses how the new Italian state functioned during its first decade, examining the problems it faced, the policies it pursued, and the economic and social progress that was made. Overall, the chapter enables you to assess whether life improved for Italians, and therefore whether unification had been worthwhile. It is split into the following sections:

- The Kingdom of Italy
- Social and economic problems

Key dates

1861	March	The Kingdom of Italy was proclaimed
1861–5		Civil war in southern Italy
1864		*The Syllabus of Errors* published
1866		Venetia was added to Kingdom of Italy
1870	July	The Doctrine of Papal Infallibility
	October	Rome was added to Italy and became its capital

1 | The Kingdom of Italy

After the proclamation of Victor Emmanuel II as King of Italy in May 1861, Piedmont's Prime Minister d'Azeglio remarked: 'Italy is made, now we must make Italians'. It was a pertinent remark. Victor Emmanuel II, scornful of his new subjects, who did not seem to understand that they now belonged to the 'nation' of which he was head, voiced his opinion that 'There are only two ways of governing Italians, by bayonets and by bribery'.

Key question
How did the new Kingdom of Italy function during the first decade of its existence?

Key date
The Kingdom of Italy was proclaimed: March 1861

The Kingdom of Italy 1859–70. Dates in brackets indicate when each state was unified with Piedmont.

Annexed to Piedmont April 1860

Ceded to France and passed to Italy by Napoleon III July 1866

N

SAVOY

LOMBARDY (1860)

TO FRANCE 1860

Magenta Solferino

VENETIA (1860)

AUSTRIA

• Turin

Custozza

FRANCE

PIEDMONT

TO FRANCE NICE 1860

ROMAGNA (1860)

OTTOMAN EMPIRE

PARMA (1860)

LUCCA

MODENA (1860)

TUSCANY (1860)

PAPAL STATES (1860)

KINGDOM OF SARDINIA-PIEDMONT

CORSICA (FRENCH)

Adriatic Sea

New capital of Italy 1870

• Rome (1870)

Naples

SARDINIA

Patrimony of St Peter all that was left to Pope by 1870

NAPLES (1860)

0   150

km

KINGDOM OF THE TWO SICILIES (1860)

Palermo

• Aspromonte

SICILY

Mediterranean Sea

Garibaldi defeated and wounded 1862

The road to political unification

Key question
What were the steps by which unification was completed after 1861?

In March 1861 the new Kingdom of Italy was officially proclaimed. Yet unification was not complete. Not until 1866 was Venetia successfully won back from Austria with the help of Napoleon III of France, despite Italy's poor performance in the war. Garibaldi made two unsuccessful attempts in 1862 and 1867 to invade and take Rome, but it was not until 1870 that the city became part of a united Italy when Napoleon III ordered his occupying troops to withdraw because they were needed to defend France against Prussia.

Key dates
Venetia was added to Kingdom of Italy: 1866

Rome was added to Italy and became its capital: October 1870

The city of Rome was the obvious natural capital of Italy and failure to include it in 1861 had been a grave disappointment to Italian liberals. Now, in 1870, disappointment turned to joy as Rome was at last declared the capital. Italian troops were welcomed as they marched in to replace the French garrison, which had long been an unwanted foreign presence in the city.

The Papacy

Key question
In what ways did the Papacy cause problems for the new Italian state?

Pope Pius IX did not join in the rejoicing, and his policies caused grave problems for the new Italian state.

Already, in 1860, Pius had lost the majority of the land making up the Papal States (see page 66). As worldly power began to slip from his grasp, he concentrated on strengthening his spiritual power over the Church and its members. In 1864 the man who had once been thought progressive published the controversial *Syllabus of Errors*, which, turning the Church away from the material world, condemned, among other things, 'progress, liberalism and modern civilisation'. He was also against religious toleration. In July 1870 he went further with the Doctrine of Papal Infallibility, which decreed that the Pope's spiritual judgement on matters of faith and morals could not be challenged as he was the supreme judge of truth for the Catholic Church.

The Syllabus of Errors published: 1864

Doctrine of Papal Infallibility: July 1870

Key dates

Now, three months later, Rome became the capital city of Italy and the Pope, distressed by what he called 'the triumph of disorder and the victory of wicked revolution', found himself left with only 109 acres of land making up the area called the Patrimony of Saint Peter. He retired into his palace of the Vatican, describing himself as its 'prisoner'. He was offered a state pension but refused it, and instead excommunicated Victor Emmanuel and the government.

Pius IX was determined to demonstrate his continued spiritual importance. As head of the Catholic Church, he announced that any Catholics who took part in Italian politics or worked for the new secular state would be excommunicated.

Through its beliefs, rituals and language, the Catholic Church had always been the main unifying element within the country. Now, even though Catholicism remained the state religion, those many liberal-minded Catholics who supported the new secular government but who wished also to keep the faith, found themselves in difficulties. The old balanced relationship between Church and State no longer existed. It threatened instead to become a bitter clash of personalities and values, as over the next two decades the Pope became ever more hostile to the Italian state.

Political problems

Apart from the question of the Pope, the government found itself with a number of other problems, which the poor qualities of most of Cavour's successors as prime minister during the 1860s did nothing to help. None was charismatic, none had the leadership qualities of the heroes of the *Risorgimento*, and many remained in power for only a short time. One prime minister, Luigi Farini, who suffered a mental breakdown, tried to stab the king and was removed from office after only three months, and Urbano Rattazzi became involved in Garibaldi's failed attacks on Rome in 1862 and 1867 and was forced to resign.

Key question
What political issues caused problems for the Italian government?

Nevertheless, Italian historians argue that, in their own way, members of the Italian governments in the 1860s and 1870s did good work establishing the new kingdom and that they were just as successful and important as those of earlier years. In 1928 the Italian philosopher Benedetto Croce wrote a spirited defence of these governments as made up of 'men of noble and self-sacrificing character' and 'upright and loyal gentlemen'. Other historians, however, such as the Communist Antonio Gramsci, described them as essentially undemocratic. It is easy to see why he thought this if we look at the constitution of the new state.

Key question
How dominant was Piedmont in the new Italy?

Italy's constitution

The Italy of 1861 was a constitutional monarchy, not the republic that Mazzini had dreamed about and worked for, nor a federation under the Pope as Gioberti and later Cavour and Napoleon III had proposed at Plombières. The constitution was based on Charles Albert's *Statuto* of 1848 (see page 53), and the Piedmontese example was closely followed. It was the King of Piedmont who became Italy's King, Victor Emmanuel II of Piedmont becoming Victor Emmanuel II of Italy – no matter that he was the *first* King of Italy. Ultimate constitutional power lay with the king in parliament and not 'the people' as Mazzini had hoped. As a result, Mazzini described the new Italian state as a 'sham'.

The new regime did not turn Italy into a true democracy, but only into what has been described a sham democracy. The government was made up of members of the Piedmontese nobility and of the educated middle-class minority who formed an élite, and the all-male parliament was elected by a very narrow framework of voters. These too were all male, over 25 years old, literate and tax-paying – about two per cent of the population – and most of them from northern Italy. It was not surprising that parliament consisted almost entirely of well-to-do traditionally minded liberals and was totally unrepresentative of the mass of the people.

Signs of change

However, some progress was made towards a more unified nation:

- The various legal codes, or collections of laws, of individual states were formed into a single criminal code based on that of Piedmont and quickly introduced everywhere except Tuscany, which kept its own moderate code. In 1865 a single system of civil law, similar to France's *Code Napoléon*, was adopted throughout the country. It allowed civil marriage, although divorce remained illegal.
- During the 1860s a unified Italian army was formed out of the old armies of Piedmont, Naples and the central Italian states, plus Garibaldi's 'Army of the South'. The whole army was modernised and reorganised along Prussian lines.
- The navies of Piedmont and Naples were amalgamated into a single force, although not until 1876 was there any attempt at modernising or reorganising it.
- Schools and universities came under state control as part of a policy to provide a unified system of education throughout the peninsula.

Summary diagram: The Kingdom of Italy

2 | Social and Economic Problems

North and south

The government was faced with serious geographical, social, political and economic problems by the need to unite two very different areas of the country: the prosperous, semi-industrialised 'advanced' north, comprising Piedmont and her immediate neighbours, and the poor, agriculturally based 'backward' south, the regions to the south of the Papal States.

Cavour had realised the enormous problems involved in uniting northern and southern in Italy, claiming that that 'To harmonise the north with the south is more difficult than to fight Austria or to struggle with Rome'.

Key question
What were the main contrasts between northern and southern Italy?

The land question

The new government in the north at first tried to deal with the problem by ignoring it. When that did not work it used the quite unsuitable solution of forcing a Piedmontese style of government on the south. It was unsuitable because, in Naples and Sicily, the problems were not so much political as social and economic. The majority of the population was illiterate, and lived in poverty and squalor, at a level of near starvation.

As the small number of great landowners continued to enclose land to add to their estates, known as **Latifundia**, there was less and less land left available for the peasants. When the old **common land** disappeared into the great estates, peasant families could not feed themselves as they had done before, for they did not now have land on which to graze cattle or to grow crops.

Key question
Why did so much common land disappear?

Latifundia
Large estates (from the Latin *latus* meaning wide, and *fundus* meaning estate).

Common land
Land held 'in common' by the people, without individual owners.

Key terms

Key question
Why was violence so
common in the
1860s?

Key date

Civil war in southern
Italy: 1861–5

Key term

Mafia
An organised
criminal gang,
originating as a
secret society in
thirteenth-century
Sicily. In the
nineteenth century
it took this name
(meaning 'swank')
and virtually ruled
parts of the island,
sometimes
protecting ordinary
peasants from the
oppression of
corrupt police
forces and judges.

Law and order

The government again showed its total lack of understanding of
the situation by introducing higher taxation. The cost of living
rose and the quality of peasant life fell even lower as they
struggled to pay the new taxes. Their life was further complicated
by new, difficult-to-understand legal systems and, worst of all, by
conscription which took the young men away from the farms
where they were needed. In 1861 around 25,000 of them took to
the hills of Naples and Sicily to avoid military service. They
scraped a living as bandits instead. Many in the west of Sicily
joined the **Mafia** which, taking advantage of the general social
unrest, was thriving, as public opinion in the south turned not
just against the landowners but also against Victor Emmanuel II
and Piedmont.

Peasant families began migrating to the towns in search of work
and, often finding none, became part of the growing underclass
of semi-destitute people whose only hope of food and shelter was
to turn to crime. This was particularly the case in Palermo, the
capital of Sicily, and in the overcrowded city of Naples, where the
respectable citizens were 'put in fear of their lives' by half-starved
beggars.

Civil war

In the early 1860s law and order, never very strong in Sicily and
Naples, broke down totally. Bandits became bolder and more
numerous as rural discontent fuelled a revolution which soon
turned into a civil war in which more people were killed than
in all the revolutions and wars of the unification period.
A Piedmontese army of some 100,000 men was called in to
suppress the disorder. It took them over four years, from
1861 to 1865, to do so.

Government reactions

Government ministers still made no real attempt to understand
what was happening in the south. Naples, they believed, was
'rotten'. Neapolitans were 'barbarians': idle, politically corrupt
and backward. They brought their troubles on themselves by their
laziness, sitting about in the sun instead of working. At the root of
the government's attitude was belief in the rightness of Cavour's
original plan to reorganise the whole peninsula on the
Piedmontese model, and in the idea that the south held great
wealth, just waiting for the north to take and use it. On both
counts they were wrong, and attempts to put them into practice
only had the effect of increasing the growth of industry in the
north while making matters socially and economically worse in
the south. Throughout the 1860s north and south remained as
far apart as ever.

The standard of living

Living standards fell throughout Italy for all social classes as the government struggled to balance the books. In the mid-1860s, when Venetia was added to the kingdom, the government's total spending exceeded its income by 60 per cent.

The level of taxation was decided not by parliament but by the king alone, and unfortunately his main interest was in making war, the most expensive activity any country can indulge in. To pay for his military activities taxes had to rise, and in 1868 the unpopular tax on grinding corn was revived. The increased taxes fell most heavily on peasants, who could least afford to pay. Many, finding that they could not survive on the produce of their few acres, moved into the towns, as large numbers of others had done before them.

Key question
How did government policies increase poverty?

The place of women

Extensive research has been done on this topic in recent decades by Italian historians. After unification, women found themselves at first, as they had been before, second-class citizens in a macho society, both in the home, where in all social classes a wife was legally subject to her husband, and in the workplace, where working women were actively discouraged from joining the new **mutual-aid societies** which were the forerunners of trade unions. In 1862 only about 10,000 women, as opposed to about 100,000 men, were members, and women continued to be paid half as much as men for the same work and the same long hours.

In the 1860s in the towns, the availability of cheap housing close to factories, which is where most of the work was available, became very important to working women. They were no longer restricted to outwork in the home or to labouring in quarries, in fields or on the roads. Until the 1870s women continued to work at home, especially once the **treadle** sewing machine came into use, but increasing numbers of women moved into the factories.

Key question
How were women exploited in this period?

Mutual-aid societies
Organisations formed by workers who pooled their resources to provide some financial benefits in times of hardship.

Treadle
A foot-operated lever that applies power to a machine.

Women's work

For many the work was making cigars, a job done exclusively by women. In one of the 20 state-owned factories, 500 workers produced 700 kilograms of cigars a day. The hours were long and the pay was low, but there was company in the rows of workers sitting side by side on high stools in the large, warm rooms. Yet there was widespread tuberculosis, caused by the overcrowded and unsanitary housing of the poor and by the fact that workers were undernourished. There was no treatment. It only needed one infected woman to be working in an unventilated workroom and dozens alongside her would catch the disease. Factory records show that hundreds of women on their books died from tuberculosis.

Unfortunately almost every job women turned their hands to brought them illness and deformity, whether it was making leather gloves on a cumbersome sewing machine, which meant hours of working in a cramped position; or catching a fever standing in dirty and cold stagnant water up to their waists for hours at a time soaking flax and hemp ready for spinning; or working along with their children in the newly planted rice fields of Piedmont and Lombardy, their feet and legs in muddy water from one hour after dawn until one hour before sunset as they tended the rice plants. As a result, death from malaria was common among the rice workers.

Working in hazardous conditions in the factories seemed preferable to many women. In Piedmont alone 36,000 women worked in the silk industry in factories where their hands were ruined by boiling water in the process of reeling the silk thread off the cocoons.

The old domestic standbys of spinning and weaving came to an end when competition from the new cotton cloth imports shook the textile industry to its foundations and led to change. From the late 1860s onwards, cloth production moved into the factory and into the machine age, producing unexpected effects on family life.

The family unit

Spinning and weaving in the home had previously involved the whole family, bringing together men, women and children. Factory work destroyed the family as a self-contained production unit and changed the division of labour between men and women. As a result, there was a great increase in the number of babies left at the foundling hospitals to free their mothers for work.

The introduction of mechanised looms in the factories eliminated the heavy work of weaving previously done by men. They found themselves no longer needed and were replaced as weavers by women and girls who were cheaper to employ, often leaving the men without work. This disturbed the long-accepted social relationships within peasant and other working families because, for the first time on any large scale, male domination was challenged as women became independent wage-earners outside the home.

Conclusion

The majority of Italians, men as well as women, must have wondered what was so wonderful about a self-governing and united Italy, as their lot remained arduous and poverty stricken. Was this really the glorious *Risorgimento* they had heard about?

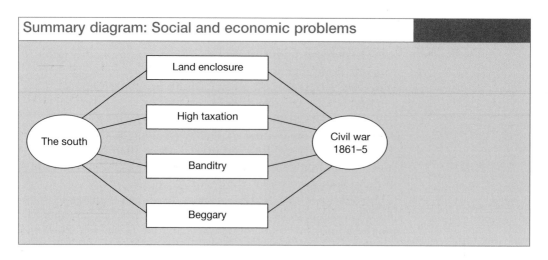

Summary diagram: Social and economic problems

Study Guide: AS Questions

In the style of AQA

(a) Explain why Italy was not fully unified until 1870. (12 marks)

(b) 'Italy was a strong new state in 1870.' Explain why you agree or disagree with this view. (24 marks)

Exam tips

The cross-references are intended to take you straight to the material that will help you to answer the questions.

(a) You should try to provide a variety of factors to explain why it took so long to unite Italy. You may wish to draw on material from earlier chapters to explain the underlying divisions within Italy that had made unification difficult and you could allude briefly to the limited nature of Cavour's aims and the position of Garibaldi by 1860. You would also need to explain the unique heritage of Venetia and the Papal States where French troops were determined to protect the Pope. You should also include the specific factors that led to the incorporation of Venetia (pages 114–15) and Rome (pages 115–16) and the importance of war.

Try to prioritise and show the links between the reasons you have chosen, perhaps distinguishing between the long- and short-term factors. You should ensure that your answer leads towards a clear and well-supported conclusion.

(b) This question is asking you to consider the strength of the new Italian state of 1870. You should make a list of points that agree with the statement and another list that disagrees. There are a number of points in this chapter which suggest the new Italian state was actually quite weak, but do ensure you think of some positive points too. By choosing one side over the other and by balancing one set of points against the other you will produce a balanced answer.

In support of the statement you might include:

- a newly united nation with plenty of potential for the future
- united legal codes
- a united army and navy offering the possibility of new military strength
- a single and expanding education system
- a broadly democratic constitution.

Disagreeing with the statement you might include:

- the degree of poverty that existed
- the position of the Papacy
- the inadequacy of the political system
- problems of law and order
- land issues and the north/south divide.

In the style of Edexcel

How far were the Italian governments successful in their attempts to deal with the problems they faced in the period 1861–70? (30 marks)

> ### Exam tips
>
> *The cross-references are designed to take you straight to the material that will help you to answer the question.*
>
> A logical approach to this question is, first, to identify the problems of the period and, then, to see how successful Italian governments were at tackling them. Your answer might include the following areas:
>
> - Unifying the whole peninsula. Clearly there was success here, in that first Venetia and then Rome became part of the Italian Kingdom. But how far was this due to the efforts of the governments, and how far to luck (see pages 114–16 and 125)?
> - Devising a satisfactory constitution for Italy. Did the 'solution' adopted work effectively? How far was it too centred on the model of Piedmont to arouse the support and enthusiasm of the whole Italian population (see pages 126–7)?
> - Securing co-operation between north and south. Did the policies coming from the politicians in the north help the position of southerners? Why was there a civil war in the south (see pages 128–9)?
> - Problems with the Church. Did governments manage to achieve a satisfactory relationship between the state and the Catholic Church (see pages 125–6)?
> - The standard of living. Did life become better for the majority of Italians? How did the position of women change (see pages 130–1)?
>
> Your answer should end with a short conclusion, in which you weigh up the successes and failures. What overall verdict will you deliver?

In the style of OCR

Study the four sources and then answer **both** sub-questions. It is recommended that you spend two-thirds of your time in answering part **(b)**.

(a) Study Sources B and C.
   Compare these sources as evidence for the attitudes of Neapolitans to unification.   (30 marks)
(b) Study all the sources.
   Use your own knowledge to assess how far the sources support the interpretation that Piedmont imposed its authority on Italy from 1860 to 1870 by force of arms.   (70 marks)

Source A

A cartoon published in Punch, *17 November 1860 comments on Garibaldi's offer of the Kingdom of Naples to Victor Emmanuel in October 1860.*

'RIGHT LEG IN THE BOOT AT LAST.' Garibaldi [kneeling] says, 'If it won't go on Sire, try a little more gunpowder.'

Source B

From: Maxime du Camp, Review of Two Worlds, *published in 1862. A Frenchman comments on the reactions of Neapolitans to the creation of Italy.*

Neapolitans recognise that Italy has no real capital and no proper frontier to the northeast where it is occupied by an enemy power. Neapolitans accept that improving reforms will follow, but first the government in Piedmont must be helped to make the nation. Everyone is now an Italian and feels it. In 1860, after Garibaldi's arrival at Naples, people at first saw him as just a new master and asked 'What is Italy and what does unity mean?' But I have spoken to many people, including sailors and peasants, and all of them know about Italian unity.

Source C

From: Giacinto De Sivo, Neapolitans in the Eyes of Civilised Nations, *published in 1862. A Neapolitan challenges the claims of Piedmont that they have liberated the Kingdom of Naples.*

Piedmont has a thirst for power, a desire to destroy and rule. The unity boasted by Piedmont is a lie. Piedmont proclaims 'Away with the Austrian!', yet she enables another foreigner, the French, to penetrate into the heart of Italian lands. Piedmont cries 'Italy!', and makes war on Italians; because she does not want to make Italy – she wants to eat Italy. Our homeland, Naples, is not hostile to Italy but fights against those who say 'Unite Italy in order to rob her'. Naples wants to unite Italy so that she can advance civilisation, not retreat into barbarity.

Source D

From: Graham Darby, The Unification of Italy, *published in 2001. A modern historian considers the nature of Italy after 1860.*

There seemed to be no alternative to Piedmontisation if Italy was to be prevented from falling apart. Piedmont's institutions were imposed on the peninsula. The Piedmontese constitution was extended to all Italy. The legal system was unified and imposed on all, except Tuscany, by 1865. Piedmont's religious laws formally separated Church and State and inspired the Pope to issue a decree in 1868 forbidding all Catholics to participate in the life of the new state. A unified Italian army was created, including in its number Neapolitan officers.

Source: adapted from OCR, January 2005

Exam tips

Read the 'General Introduction' section at the start of the study guide in Chapter 2, page 46.

(a) There is plenty here to use to consider how Sources B and C offer evidence on Neapolitan attitudes. One mistake would be to read Sources B and C as real alternatives. If you look closely, Source C has elements that favour unification (and Naples' position in the new Italy) and are in agreement that unification is incomplete. Beyond that common ground is where they diverge. Source B sees the French as the obstacle whereas for Source C it is the Austrians. Equally, they take different views of Piedmont as a help or hindrance to unification. You should also note the tone of each; Source B is optimistic about the future for Italy whereas Source C is pessimistic, seeing Naples as being exploited and in danger of suffering. The situation in Naples at that time (e.g. brigands, expectations after the fall of the Bourbons) might help to explain this scepticism.

(b) Read the question carefully. What do you have to do? The instruction tells you to *use your own knowledge* – to do what? You have to use it to assess how far the sources support an interpretation on Piedmont's behaviour during the decade 1860–70. So if you write a general answer on Italian unification, and/or write about Garibaldi's earlier exploits in the south, you will score low marks. To 'stay on message' and answer the question, mark those key phrases with a highlighter pen, and re-read them from time to time.

   You could start with Source A because it seems to agree with the view given in the question. Garibaldi's victories were achieved in Victor Emmanuel's name, and the cartoon suggests that gunpowder (more force) will be needed to unite Italy properly. Before you sift your knowledge of events in the south in 1860 to see how far that view is supported by the facts, and bring in Sources C and D for further corroboration, look again at Source A. Is that the view that it puts forward?

   Garibaldi has put down his sword. Look again at the opinions of Sources B and D on the view put forward in the question: Piedmont imposing its authority by force of arms. According to Source B, Piedmont was a benign power that had the interests of Italy at heart, building the new Italy through progressive reforms. As for the view of Source D, Darby points out that Piedmont was not able to impose its authority in either Naples or Rome on some issues. Further, the means by which Piedmont would be imposing its authority – the new Italian army – is shown in Source D to have been much more than a Piedmontese force. Ask yourself one final question about the 1860s. If force was the key element during those years, was it even Italian? Was it French force that acquired Venetia and Rome for a Piedmontese-led Italy?

7 Conclusion: The *Risorgimento* and Italian Unification

POINTS TO CONSIDER

This final chapter provides you with an opportunity to reflect on the contents of the book as a whole and to review the process of unification. It focuses on:

- Mazzini's view of the Kingdom of Italy
- Historians and the *Risorgimento*
- The 'heroes' of the *Risorgimento*

By the end of the chapter you should be in a position to make up your own mind on the key issues, particularly on how important the *Risorgimento* was in the unification of Italy, and on what combination of factors actually led to unification.

1 | Mazzini's View of the Kingdom of Italy

In 1871 Mazzini, who had hoped for so long for a free and united Italy, criticised the 10-year-old Kingdom of Italy in outspoken terms:

Key question
How valid are Mazzini's criticisms of the new Italian state?

> The Italy which we represent today, like it or not, is a living lie. Not only do foreigners own Italian territory on our frontiers with France and Germany, but even if we possessed Nice and Trieste, we should still have only … the dead corpse of Italy.
>
> Italy was put together just as though it were a piece of lifeless mosaic, and the battles which made this mosaic were fought by foreign rulers who should have been loathed as our common enemies. Lombardy, scene of the great Five Days in 1848, allowed herself to be joined to Italy by a French despot. The Venetians, despite their heroic defence in 1849, come to us by kind permission of a German monarch. The best of us once fought against France for possession of Rome … Southern Italy was won by volunteers and a real movement of the people, but then it resigned its early promise and gave in to a government which still refuses to give Italy a new national constitution.
>
> The battles fought by Italy in this process were defeats … Italians are now without a new constitution that could express their will. We can therefore have no real national existence or international policy of our own. In domestic politics … we are governed by a few rich men … Ordinary people are disillusioned. They had watched … as

Italy, once ruler of the civilised world, began to rise again; but now they turn away their eyes and say to themselves: 'this is just the ghost of Italy'.

Mazzini's motives

Why was Mazzini so critical of the new kingdom? Perhaps he was simply resentful of the fact that, as a still suspect revolutionary republican, he was not allowed to take the seat in parliament to which he had been elected. Perhaps he was out of touch, living emotionally in the 1840s. After all, some of his hopes had been fulfilled. He might fret about the loss of Italian-speaking Nice, but at least the Austrians had gone, Lombardy and Venetia were back in Italian hands and Rome had become the capital city.

Yet there was also justice in Mazzini's comments. What disappointed him was partly the way Italy had been united. Italy had not 'made herself' as he and others had hoped, but had needed foreign help. In a sense, therefore, 'Italy' had been unified prematurely, before a common struggle had first created 'Italians'. He was also highly critical of the present state of the country. Italy was free and the states were united politically but they were not united socially or economically. The division between the prosperous north and the impoverished south had not been resolved. Also, Italy was a monarchy not a republic and, although the kingdom was a secular one, Italian life was still overshadowed by the spiritual, if not the temporal, power of the Catholic Church.

Mazzini argued that Italians had had no opportunity to create a new constitution and a new lifestyle. The strong political position of Piedmont in 1860 had enabled Cavour and his successors to force Piedmont's king and constitution on the rest of Italy, along with a liberal government. Mazzini did not quarrel with the exclusion of women as voters or candidates for election: he believed that they should stay quietly at home as daughters, wives and mothers to men and have no political or public role. But he was concerned that most of the male population, by not being allowed to vote or to stand as candidates, had been excluded from decision-making and had therefore no good reason to support the new state.

True democracy (rule by the people), which Mazzini had promised members of 'Young Italy', was as far away as ever. In his view the spirit of the *Risorgimento* was dead, killed by Piedmont's politicians. This is a view that has created much controversy among historians.

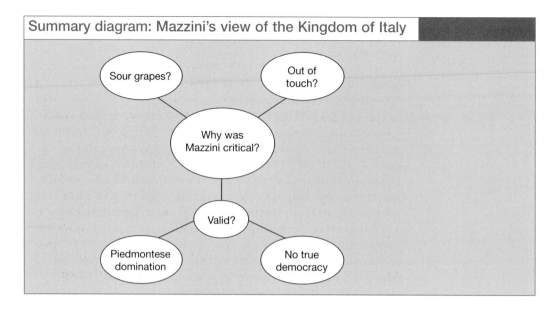

Summary diagram: Mazzini's view of the Kingdom of Italy

2 | The Key Debate: Historians and the *Risorgimento*

In what sense, if any, does the concept of the *Risorgimento* explain the unification of Italy?

Both Italian and non-Italian historians have over the years developed theories about the importance or otherwise of the *Risorgimento* and have tried to define exactly what it was. While some historians see it as the mainspring of the unification movement, others have questioned whether it was ever an actual movement or only a nineteenth-century myth created by the ruling élite to justify, and thus maintain, their domination.

Italian and British views
Italian interpretations

In Italy, the belief in the *Risorgimento* as a revolutionary movement has tended to be strong. The term has often been defined as active 'resurgence' or 'national rebirth' driven by nationalist ideals of unity and independence, based on a national memory of past glory and the hope of an equally glorious future. The unification of Italy was thus heroic and magnificent.

Most Italians continue to see it as a movement in which Italy found itself as the result of a long campaign dominated by the larger-than-life patriotic leaders: Cavour, Garibaldi, Victor Emmanuel II and Mazzini. It is believed that these men acting together, with the aid of Napoleon III of France, gave Italy unity and independence. Rivalries between the heroes of the *Risorgimento* are played down as no more than temporary squabbles resulting from war, and as such they do nothing to alter the fact that the events of 1860–1 were the great romantic climax to a long process of national development and growth which gave Italy back its soul.

Key question
In what ways have Italian and British historians differed in their major interpretations?

Key term

Philosophers
Those who study
the nature of reality
by using logic and
abstract theories.

One problem here is that many Italian historians have also been
philosophers, making use of rather abstruse theories and abstract
ideas in their writings. Not for them the usual bread-and-butter
of historians: concrete facts about nationalist movements, wars,
revolutions, accidents and individuals. As a result, much of their
historical writing is extremely hard to follow.

Yet it is not difficult to spot national bias, even if it is expressed
incoherently and emotionally. One moderate Italian historian
writing in 1943 described the *Risorgimento* as 'a fact or better a
process of a spiritual character, an intimate and thorough
transformation of national life … Italy and the *Risorgimento* have
both been understood over the centuries, before all else, as facts
of consciousness, as spiritual attitudes'. Another Italian historian,
writing in 1960, insisted 'the *Risorgimento* was not due to fortunate
circumstances or to selfish interests … it was a spirit of sacrifice, it
was suffering in the way of exile and in the galleys, it was the
blood of Italian youth on the battlefields … it was the passion of a
people for its Italian identity'.

British interpretations

Non-Italian historians are much more doubtful about how far, if
at all, the *Risorgimento* was important in unifying Italy. They are
even more doubtful about whether the 'heroes of the *Risorgimento*'
acted together to unite Italy and to give her independence. Ever
since G.M. Trevelyan, writing about the *Risorgimento* in the early
years of the twentieth century, suggested that it was personal
hostility and not united action that motivated the 'heroes' and
provided 'the mainsprings of action which created a unified state',
other British historians have tended to follow a similar line. In
particular Denis Mack Smith, probably the best-known British
historian writing about the *Risorgimento*, has argued with
impressive details that it was not the agreements but the
disagreements between Cavour and Garibaldi that brought about
the unification of Italy by Piedmont. Cavour united Italy not so
much because he intended to or because he thought it right to do
so, but because Garibaldi's unauthorised military successes in
southern Italy forced him into action.

There is also a fundamental difference of approach. British
historians have tended to be more down to earth and less
theoretical than Italians, drawing their interpretations from a
consideration of what actually happened, and therefore their
writings are easier to follow. Mack Smith, for instance, is practical
in that he focuses on Piedmont.

Mack Smith has argued that it was the war of 1859 against
Austria in the north, masterminded by Cavour and Napoleon III,
along with Garibaldi's military successes in the south and
Cavour's move to stop him reaching Rome in 1860, that made it
possible for Piedmont to force unification on the rest of Italy. It
was not therefore the result of some intangible 'national rebirth'
or *Risorgimento*. Yet it was at this point that misleading official
propaganda made the *Risorgimento* a part of Italy's shared past, a
myth that transformed unification into a popular quest for

national freedom and unity, rather than the result of rivalry and Piedmontese expansion.

Revisionist historians point out that national unity was only one possible result of the Italian struggle for independence. It was not inevitable. They believe that it came about because of French politics and Piedmontese policies, and not from popular nationalist pressure for a unified Italy. This may well be so.

Conclusion

Diplomacy, war and the rivalries between Cavour and Garibaldi were obviously vital factors in the unification of Italy. Nevertheless, the romantic pull of the *Risorgimento* persists and seems likely to continue to do so. Its ideals were important because they provided an emotional and political appeal, giving at least some Italians a common identity and purpose which fuelled the nationalist cause both before and after unification.

Italy was not unified solely by wars and the intrigues and rivalries of politicians. Nationalism played a part. National feeling did rouse a section of public opinion to support Piedmont's ambitions to lead a unified Italy and to provide its first king and its first national constitution. Without nationalist support a united Italy as early as 1861 would not have been possible.

Some key books in the debate
D. Beales and E. Biagini, *The Risorgimento and the Unification of Italy*, 2nd edition (Longman, 2002).
M. Clark, *The Italian Risorgimento* (Longman, 1998).
Harry Hearder, *Italy in the Age of the Risorgimento*, 1790–1870 (Longman, 1983).
Walter Maturi, *Interpretazioni del Risorgimento* (Turin, 1962).
Denis Mack Smith, *The Making of Italy* (Macmillan, 1968) and *Italy: A Modern History* (University of Michigan, 1979).
G.M. Trevelyan, *Garibaldi and the Making of Italy* (Longman, 1911).

Summary diagram: Historians and the *Risorgimento*

Did the *Risorgimento* produce unification?

YES	NO
Often Italian historians	Often British historians
Spiritual ideals	Practical realities
Intended	Unintended
Philosophical language	Ordinary language
Harmony between leading figures	Often disharmony
National feeling	International diplomacy
Italian nationalism	Piedmontese imperialism
Magnificent	Sometimes inglorious

Key question
What roles should be assigned to the leading individuals involved with Italian unification?

3 | The 'Heroes' of the *Risorgimento*

Individuals were not all-important, but they were certainly crucial, in the unification of Italy. Four Italian 'heroes' are often singled out: Cavour, Garibaldi, Victor Emmanuel and Mazzini. Yet there was also a non-Italian, the French Emperor, Napoleon III, who cannot be left out of the reckoning. What conclusions can be reached about the roles of these men?

Cavour and Garibaldi

There was indeed, as Trevelyan, Mack Smith and others suggest, hostility between Cavour and Garibaldi. How important was it? If Cavour had not distrusted Garibaldi and feared in 1860 that, after his military successes in Naples and Sicily, he might take Rome and also make himself permanent ruler of an independent southern Italy and even turn it into a republic, he would not have made the decision to invade the Papal States to prevent Garibaldi from moving against Rome. This decision led to an open quarrel between the liberal Cavour and the radical Garibaldi on the future of the Italian peninsula. It has been said, with some reason, that Cavour united Italy in order to get the better of Garibaldi, whom he still suspected of being a supporter of Mazzini.

Garibaldi, for his part, disliked Cavour personally and distrusted diplomacy. He still believed that Italy could only be united by revolutionary means, and that armed action was essential. Like the proverbial bull in a china shop, he had charged into an attack on Sicily and then Naples. After his unexpected successes there, he planned to go on to take Venetia and Rome, without considering what the results of this might be. Such action would have brought armed intervention by France to protect her garrison in Rome and probably by Austria to retain her hold on Venetia. The new and fragile Kingdom of Italy could not have withstood such a double attack.

It was Cavour's greatest contribution to unification that his invasion of the Papal States effectively prevented Garibaldi from carrying out the second part of his plan, beginning with the attack on Rome, just as it was Garibaldi's greatest contribution that he was able to carry out the first part, the conquest of Naples and Sicily, despite Cavour's opposition.

Garibaldi's willingness to surrender Naples and Sicily to Victor Emmanuel II avoided civil war and left the way clear for Cavour and Piedmont to take over Italy. Was this the act of a great and generous man laying the spoils of war at the feet of his king, or merely a way of getting out of a difficult situation, now that the fighting was over? Opinion is divided on this. Yet it seems certain that Victor Emmanuel and Cavour were determined that Garibaldi's contribution was finished and that he should now quit Italian affairs, leaving them to continue in a more diplomatic way the process of unification. With no immediate prospect of further fighting Garibaldi too seems to have been quite happy to return to the simple life on the island of Caprera.

Victor Emmanuel II

How important a role did the 'gallant king' (*Il Re galantuomo*), the first king of a united Italy, play in the unification of his new kingdom? Famous for his incredibly long and deeply cherished moustaches, he was personally popular, with his bluff and hearty manner. But of his politics it was not easy to be sure.

Despite the king's frequently coarse language, Queen Victoria, in whose honour he sacrificed 10 centimetres from his moustache, found him more attractive than she expected when he visited London in 1855: 'He is so frank, open, just, straightforward, liberal and tolerant, with much sound good sense'. Yet this was not the judgement of the French ambassador three years earlier. 'King Victor Emmanuel is in no sense liberal', he wrote; 'his tastes, his education and his whole habit of behaviour all go the other way … Nor does he like parliamentary liberties, nor a free press. He just accepts them temporarily as a kind of weapon of war.'

In popular Italian mythology, Victor Emmanuel was of vital importance. The enormous Victor Emanuel Monument in Rome (see below) embodies such a view. Yet foreign historians have been less enthusiastic, being inclined to believe that the king's only real claim to fame is that he happened to be there at the right time to become the figurehead for Italian nationalists and, after unification, for the new Kingdom of Italy. Even Garibaldi called him merely 'the symbol of our resurgence and of the prosperity of our country'. It may have been what he represented, rather than what he did, that gave Victor Emmanuel II a special place in

The splendid Victor Emmanuel Monument in Rome, built between 1885 and 1911.

Italian history. Had he not been lucky when it was generally believed, probably falsely, that he alone had defied the Austrians and maintained the constitution in 1849 (see page 55)?

Nevertheless, though his role was a subordinate one, he played an important part in unification. After all:

- it was he who appointed Cavour as prime minister in the first place
- he was keener than Cavour on joining the Crimean War
- he refused Cavour's unrealistic demand to carry on the war against Austria in 1859 after the French signed the armistice at Villafranca (see page 66)
- he allowed Cavour's return early in the following year
- against Cavour's wishes he gave some encouragement to Garibaldi in 1860.

Mazzini

Mazzini undoubtedly deserves his place in the list of 'heroes' but, unlike the others, his active contribution to Italian unification had finished long before 1861. He was the intellectual heart and mind of the nationalist movement. His great moments were in the 1830s and 1840s, when his drive for independence and unity were focused through 'Young Italy' and when, for a short time, he headed the Roman Republic.

His reputation made him too extreme, too revolutionary and, above all, too republican and anti-Catholic to be acceptable to Piedmontese liberals or to the Church, although he was not without religious beliefs, declaring for instance that God spoke, not through priests because Christianity was now outmoded, but through the people. In exile he kept in touch with what was happening in Italy through the National Society, returning occasionally in secret for short visits, but after 1849 his influence steadily waned. Even so, it was he who suggested that Garibaldi take Sicily, several months before he agreed to do so. (Garibaldi, Mazzini judged, had 'a heart of gold but the brains of an ox'.) Also, he was optimistic and flexible enough in March 1860 to endorse Victor Emmanuel as Italy's leader, since that seemed to be the popular choice.

Mazzini was more popular abroad than in Italy, due largely to Piedmontese propaganda at home which painted him as far more inflexible, dogmatic and violent than was really the case. His voluminous writings in exile – some 10,000 letters and articles – were more often read by foreigners than Italians, and sometimes their tone was mystical and their meaning unclear. But to his admirers, including his biographer, Mack Smith, he was a profound political thinker. It is certainly arguable that an Italy united by Mazzinians, if indeed that was a possibility, would have been a far more just and equal society than that which actually came about after 1860.

Napoleon III of France

Napoleon III worried a great deal about what later generations would think of him, and in France historians are still divided in their opinions of his aims, ambitions and character, not surprisingly in view of his passion for secrecy and intrigue.

Napoleon's intentions

Napoleon III's motives for involving himself in Italy are hard to fathom. But whatever they were, it can be argued that without him and his army the Austrians would not have been driven out of Lombardy in 1859. Piedmont could not have done it. Certainly nothing in their military record, including the two battles of Custoza, suggests that Piedmontese forces were likely to succeed alone against Austria. An independent and united Italy would surely have been impossible for many years longer.

Many Italians agreed with Garibaldi after the Peace of Villafranca: 'Do not forget the gratitude we owe to Napoleon III and the French army, so many of whose valiant sons have been killed or maimed for the cause of Italy'. Later, after the handing over to the French of Nice, Garibaldi's home town, he was less enthusiastic about Napoleon, whom he called 'a **vulpine knave**'. This should not lead us to underestimate the debt that Cavour and Garibaldi owed to Louis Napoleon, but neither should we overestimate it.

Vulpine
Like a fox –
cunning or sly.

Knave
A scoundrel.

Key terms

Napoleon's record

In an earlier period, Napoleon did very little to help the Italian cause. In fact, quite the opposite. In 1849 he had sent the French army to crush the Roman Republic, remaining afterwards to garrison the city and protect the Pope. At the secret meeting with Cavour at Plombières in July 1858 Napoleon's aim seems to have been not to unite Italy but to keep it divided into a federation of comparatively powerless separate states. As the war of 1859 began Napoleon proclaimed that his aims were not conquest but 'to restore Italy to the Italians'. He came, he said, in the guise of a liberator as he took command of the Franco-Piedmontese army, but unlike Napoleon I he was no military genius. After the two bloody battles of Magenta and Solferino an armistice was agreed at Villafranca in July as a result of which Austria surrendered Lombardy, via France, to Piedmont but kept Venetia. The war over, Napoleon returned to France. There he found himself the subject of criticism for his conduct of the war.

The French were not the only critics. Victor Emmanuel II and Cavour felt that Napoleon had betrayed them by going home before he had done what he promised, which was to 'free Italy to the shores of the Adriatic', in other words, to drive the Austrians out of Venetia as well as Lombardy. Napoleon made some amends in 1866 when, as a result of his complicated diplomacy, he came into possession of Venetia and quickly handed it over to the Kingdom of Italy. But his troops only finally left Rome when he was forced to withdraw them because of France's war with Prussia in 1870.

So who did unite Italy? Cavour, Garibaldi, Victor Emmanuel II, Mazzini or Napoleon III? Was it one of them? Or some of them? Or all of them?

Key question
Why was Piedmont so dominant in the movement for unification?

Piedmont

Perhaps only individual people can be heroes. But the state of Piedmont was so important in the story of Italy that we must focus briefly on its leading role.

The new united Italy became a secular constitutional monarchy rather than a republic or federation of states largely because Piedmont itself had remained politically stable as a constitutional monarchy after the failure of the 1848 revolutions. During the 1850s Piedmontese power grew. It developed:

- a strong central government
- a well-organised civil service
- and an effective army, unlike any of the other states.

It addition, it forged ahead economically, partly owing to the enlightened trade and other policies pursued by its governments. Furthermore, it had as its sons not only Victor Emmanuel II but political and military leaders, including Cavour (born in Turin) and Garibaldi (born in Nice, which became part of Piedmont in 1815), who could use diplomacy and war to best advantage.

As a power

Piedmont had also acquired a sufficiently good reputation outside Italy to be able to negotiate on a near equal footing with the Great Powers. This reputation had been earned by the decision of the king and prime minister to support French and British forces during the Crimean War. ('I am certain that the laurels which our soldiers will win on the battlefields of the east', said Cavour, justifying his decision in the Piedmontese parliament, 'will do more for the future of Italy than all those who have sought to regenerate her with the voice and with the pen'.) Piedmont had no direct interest in the war, but participation won Cavour a seat among the Great Powers at the Paris peace conference in 1856, and brought him into contact with Napoleon III.

As well as acquiring international influence Cavour was finding unexpected support within Italy. The Mazzinian National Society, which had been a republican and revolutionary movement, turned its back on its origins in 1858 and began campaigning instead, in a rather limited way, for Piedmont, arguing that all Italians should rally round Cavour and Victor Emmanuel II as long as Piedmont was ready to work wholeheartedly with the Italian people and to put Italian independence and unity first.

Piedmont the model

To many it seemed natural that, since Piedmontese leaders had played such a major role in the actual process of unification, the new Kingdom of Italy should be modelled on the Kingdom of Piedmont. Those who were uncertain of Piedmont's glorious role might be convinced by the published versions of Cavour's letters, carefully edited and sometimes fabricated in the 1860s, to show Piedmont in the best possible light, and its enemies – the Pope, the King of Naples and Mazzini (ironically a son of Piedmont himself, being born in Genoa) – in the worst. Surely it was only right that Italy should have a constitution and civil service, as well as a legal and financial system, based closely on that of gallant Piedmont? Those who disagreed had no choice in the matter, especially since the army was controlled by Piedmont.

Conclusion

Key question
What problems faced the new Italian state in 1861?

In 1861, Piedmont's Prime Minister d'Azeglio had remarked: 'Italy is made, now we must make Italians'. It seems appropriate to end with another less often quoted remark which shows that he at least was aware of the long and difficult task that lay ahead for the government in 1861. It took a long time to achieve unification, and many had hoped that it would come about earlier, during the revolutions of 1848–9 if not before. But d'Azeglio realised that much more time was needed when he said: 'To make an Italy out of Italians, one must not be in a hurry'.

Despite the rhetoric of the *Risorgimento*, Italy was still a country with strong local loyalties and identities. People did not automatically become 'Italians' in 1861 or 1866 or 1870 just because they lived in Italy. They remained first and foremost Piedmontese, Neapolitans, Tuscans, Lombards or Venetians. To make Italy into a single nation was going to be a slow process. Unification, so long awaited, was no more than a first step.

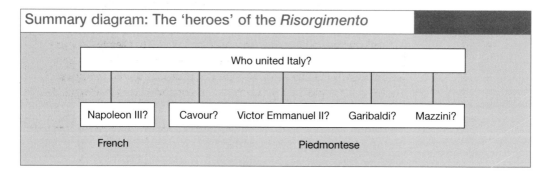

Summary diagram: The 'heroes' of the *Risorgimento*

Study Guide: AS Question

In the style of Edexcel

How far do you agree that it was mainly because of Cavour's modernisation of Piedmont before 1858 that Piedmont was able to play such a key role in the unification of Italy?   (30 marks)

Exam tips

The cross-references are designed to take you straight to the material that will help you to answer the question.

Cavour's modernisation of Piedmont was a precondition for unification. Without it unification could not have been achieved in the way that it was (see pages 56–7 and 147).

- Why was Piedmont in a position by 1858 to spearhead unification in northern Italy? How strong was the state, compared with other Italian states? What political, economic and military advantages did it enjoy? What diplomatic traditions had it established (see pages 55–9 and 147)?
- What actions did the government of Piedmont take in 1858–60 that helped to bring about unification (see pages 59–67)? There is a danger here that you may be tempted to give a narrative. Hence you must focus squarely on the key actions that led to unification, especially the war of 1859 and the invasion of the Papal States in 1860 to prevent Garibaldi attacking Rome. Clearly Piedmont's 'important role' was due in part to the actions of its prime minister, in winning French support and in reacting boldly to the unexpected initiatives of others.

Which factor do you think deserves most weight? Clearly Cavour's role is significant in Piedmont's prominence, but what was most significant – his modernisation programme, or will you give more weight to his diplomacy? Or to his decision to invade the Papal States in 1860 perhaps?

The Sheffield College

Hillsborough LRC
Telephone: 0114 260 2254

Further Reading

There are a number of helpful books for students wanting to know more about this period of Italian history.

There are many general textbooks that place Italian unification into its contemporary context, but perhaps the most useful is:

J.A.S. Grenville, *Europe Reshaped 1848–1878*, 2nd edition (Fontana, 2000).

This is solid, reliable and readable. It also has a good section on the relations between Cavour and Garibaldi.

Among the books specifically on Italian unification, the best is still probably:

H. Hearder, *Italy in the Age of the* Risorgimento *1790–1870* (Longman, 1983).

It not only deals clearly with political events but provides useful and interesting background reading on literature and the arts, on religious issues and economic and social conditions. The chapters on Piedmont and on Cavour are particularly helpful. There is also a section on sources and the evidence they provide for the unification of Italy.

Among other books, the following are recommended:

D. Beales and E. Biagini, *The* Risorgimento *and the Unification of Italy*, 2nd edition (Longman, 2002).
L. Riall, *The Italian* Risorgimento (Routledge, 1994).
M. Clark, *The Italian* Risorgimento (Longman, 1998).
D. Mack Smith, *The Making of Italy* (Macmillan, 1968) and *Italy: A Modern History* (University of Michigan, 1979).

A good starting point for the study of Napoleon III and his contribution to Italian unification is:

Roger Price, *Napoleon III and the Second Empire* (Routledge, 1997).

For those wishing to know more about the Austrian Empire, another book in the *Access to History* series is recommended:

Nick Pelling, *The Habsburg Empire 1815–1918* (Hodder & Stoughton, 1996).

A very useful short account of how a united Italy fared during its first decade may be found in:

Christopher Duggan, 'Nation-building in 19th-century Italy', *History Today*, February 2002, pp. 9–15.

Among biographies, the following are valuable:

J. Ridley, *Garibaldi* (Constable, 1974).
Denis Mack Smith, *Cavour* (Weidenfeld and Nicolson, 1985) and *Mazzini* (Yale, 1994).
Harry Hearder, *Cavour* (Pearson, 2000).

Sources on the unification of Italy

Two short but very valuable collections of source material are:

Vyvyen Brendon, *The Making of Modern Italy* 1800–71 (Hodder & Stoughton, 1998).
Michael Morrogh, *The Unification of Italy*, 2nd edition (Palgrave, 2002).

Glossary

Absolute monarchy A political system under which a monarch rules without a constitution that limits his powers and without a parliament whose agreement is needed for the making of laws.

Ambivalence Contradictory ideas or feelings.

Annexation The act of taking possession of land and adding it to one's own territory.

Anticlerical Unsympathetic or hostile to the Church and its clergy.

Armistice A truce, or ceasefire.

Breech-loading rifles Rifles whose bullets are loaded through the chamber (or breech) rather than through the barrel (or muzzle). They could be fired four or five times more quickly than muzzle-loaders, and soldiers could load them lying down.

Carbonari Means 'charcoal burners' in Italian (the singular being *Carbonaro*), and it has been suggested that the earliest members were men who sold charcoal for domestic fuel. Soon, however, middle-class members predominated.

Ceded Officially handed over.

Civil marriage Marriage without a church service.

Clericalist Supporting the Catholic Church, its clergy and its policies.

Code Napoléon A set of civil laws, formulated in 1804, which gave France a single legal system and attempted to promote the principle of equal rights for all citizens. (Women, it should be noted, were classified as minors not as citizens.)

Common land Land held 'in common' by the people, without individual owners.

Confederation A loose alliance of states.

Congress A meeting of several countries to settle key issues.

Conscripted Forcibly enlisted into the army.

Constituente A meeting in Rome of representatives from all over Italy.

Constitutional monarchy A system under which a king is bound by certain agreed restrictions on his power set out in a written document (the constitution).

Contingent Subject to chance and to the effects of the unforeseen.

Counter-revolutionary Bringing about a revolution that is opposed to or reverses a former revolution.

Coup A sudden and violent seizure of power.

Crimean War A war fought between Britain and France, with some support from Piedmont, against Russia. Austria decided to remain neutral.

Customs union An economic agreement whereby two or more states agree to lower or eliminate taxes on the goods they trade with each other.

Dialect The form of a language found in a particular region.

Dictator Originally a term used in Ancient Rome to denote a chief magistrate with absolute power, appointed in an emergency.

Dowry Property or money presented by a bride or her family to her husband.

Dynasty A succession of powerful rulers from the same family.

Élite The most important and influential groups in a society, usually those who are wealthy and well educated.

Excommunicated   Excluded from the services and sacraments of the Catholic Church. Those who died excommunicated could not be buried by a priest or in consecrated ground, and so, it was commonly believed, would go to hell.

Expeditionary force   A small army dispatched for a particular mission.

Federal   Possessing states that are self-governing in their internal affairs.

Foundling   An infant abandoned by its mother and cared for by others.

Freemasonry   A secret fraternity providing fellowship and mutual assistance.

French Revolution   In the 'great revolution', beginning in 1789, the existing order was overthrown and a republic set up, Louis XVI being executed in 1793.

Garibaldini   The soldiers of Garibaldi, also known as legionaries and Red Shirts.

Garrison   A body of troops stationed to defend a town or locality.

Genoa   The Vienna Settlement of 1815 gave Piedmont control of the former republic of Genoa. This was of great commercial benefit to Piedmont, as Genoa was an important port. But the Genoese were far from impressed, resenting the loss of their former political and commercial independence.

Ghettos   Special quarters in Italian towns outside which Jews were forbidden to live.

Guerrilla fighters   Small independent groups, using unorthodox tactics, fighting against regular troops.

Hair shirt   A garment made of haircloth, causing discomfort to the body and thereby, according to believers, bringing its wearer closer to God.

Imperialistic   Motivated by the desire to dominate or capture other people's territory.

Inquisition   A much-feared tribunal for prosecuting and punishing heresy, founded in the thirteenth century.

Jesuits   Members of the Society of Jesus, a religious order founded in the sixteenth century, who were feared for their extreme loyalty to the Papacy.

Knave   A scoundrel.

Latifundia   Large estates (from the Latin *latus* meaning wide, and *fundus* meaning estate).

Lay population   People who are not members of the clergy.

Legion   The name taken by Garibaldi's irregular troops. Originally it was a division of 3000–6000 men in the army of Ancient Rome. Individual members were called legionaries.

Liberals   Members of the élite who wanted progressive change: often constitutional government, the guarantee of individual freedoms and free trade.

Mafia   An organised criminal gang, originating as a secret society in thirteenth-century Sicily. In the nineteenth century it took this name (meaning 'swank') and virtually ruled parts of the island, sometimes protecting ordinary peasants from the oppression of corrupt police forces and judges.

Merchant navy   A country's commercial shipping fleet.

Minister of the Interior   The European equivalent of the British Home Secretary, the minister responsible for, among other things, police and internal security.

Mobilised   Organised for a possible war.

Mutual-aid societies   Organisations formed by workers who pooled their resources to provide some financial benefits in times of hardship.

National Society   A body set up in 1856 by moderate republicans, aiming to bridge the gap between Mazzini and Garibaldi. Led by the Venetian Daniele Manin, it began to look to the Piedmontese monarchy to spearhead unification.

Naval blockade The use of ships to prevent people or goods entering or leaving ports.

Outworkers Those provided with work by a factory but doing it at home.

Pellagra A disease causing skin complaints, diarrhoea and madness that often ends in suicide.

Philosophers Those who study the nature of reality by using logic and abstract theories.

Poncho A circular cape-like garment with no sleeves or fastenings, and merely a hole for the head.

Progressive Forward-looking, favouring reform.

Quadrilateral A group of four heavily defended fortresses near the Austrian border (in Mantua, Peschiera, Verona and Legnago).

Radicals Reformers who wanted greater change than the liberals, including the overthrow of monarchies.

Reactionary Favouring a return to previous political conditions and being opposed to political progress.

Red Cross An international agency founded in 1864 to assist those who were wounded or captured in wars.

Regent A person appointed to administer a state whose monarch is unable to do so.

Republican democracy A system under which an elected government controls the affairs of a state, and in which there is no monarch, even as a figurehead.

Restored Monarchs The rulers whom the Congress of Vienna allowed to return to Italy.

Revisionist historians Those who disagree with generally accepted historical interpretations and seek to overturn them by arguing differently.

Risorgimento The word first came into use at the end of the eighteenth century and means 'resurgence' or 'rebirth'. Those who first used it suggested that Italian unification would be a noble and heroic affair, paralleling glorious episodes in Italian history such as the Roman Empire and the Renaissance.

Satellites Weak states dependent on or controlled by a more powerful country.

Second front An alternative scene of battle, generally diverting the enemy's attention from the major focus of a war.

Secularist One who favours the state over the Church.

Spiritual authority The religious power of the Pope, as head of the Catholic Church.

Temporal power The worldly authority of the Pope, as ruler of the Papal States.

Trade guilds Associations of craftsmen; early forms of trade unions.

Treadle A foot-operated lever that applies power to a machine.

Triumvirate A governing group of three men.

Viceroy A ruler exercising authority on behalf of a king or queen.

Vulpine Like a fox – cunning or sly.

Xenophobia Hatred of foreigners.

Index